PENGUIN BOOKS

Monster

Allan Hall is a foreign correspondent based in Berlin working for various publications around the world, including the *Daily Mail* in London, the *Age* in Melbourne, Australia, the *Scotsman* in Edinburgh and the *New York Post* in the USA. Formerly the bureau chief for Britain's biggest-selling newspapers – the *Sun* and then the *Daily Mirror* – in New York, he has been based in Germany, covering central Europe, for the past decade.

He is also the author of twenty books on crime and history.

D0230429

Monster

ALLAN HALL

PENGUIN BOOKS

PENGUIN BOOKS

Published by the Penguin Group
Penguin Books Ltd, 80 Strand, London WC2R ORL, England
Penguin Group (USA) Inc., 375 Hudson Street, New York, New York 10014, USA
Penguin Group (Canada), 90 Eglinton Avenue East, Suite 700, Toronto, Ontario, Canada M4P 2Y3
(a division of Pearson Penguin Canada Inc.)
Penguin Ireland, 25 St Stephen's Green, Dublin 2, Ireland
(a division of Penguin Books Ltd)
Penguin Group (Australia), 250 Camberwell Road, Camberwell, Victoria 3124, Australia
(a division of Pearson Australia Group Pty Ltd)
Penguin Books India Pvt Ltd, 11 Community Centre, Panchsheel Park, New Delhi – 110 017, India
Penguin Group (NZ), 67 Apollo Drive, Rosedale, North Shore 0632, New Zealand
(a division of Pearson New Zealand Ltd)
Penguin Books (South Africa) (Pty) Ltd, 24 Sturdee Avenue, Rosebank, Johannesburg 2196, South Africa

Penguin Books Ltd, Registered Offices: 80 Strand, London WC2R ORL, England

www.penguin.com

First published 2008
1

Copyright © Allan Hall and Central European News Ltd, 2008
All rights reserved

Picture credits: Europics for pictures 1, 2, 3, 4, 5, 9, 10, 14, 17, 18, 21, 23, 25, 26, 28, 31;
Europics / Paul Plutsch for pictures 6, 7, 8, 20, 24, 27; Europics / LKA NÖ (Landeskriminalamt
Niederösterreich) for pictures 11, 12, 13, 30; Europics / Thomas Leitner for pictures 15, 16;
Europics / Elisabeth Storer for picture 19; Europics / Fritz Schimke for picture 22;
Europics / LKA OÖ (Landeskriminalamt Oberösterreich) for picture 29.

The moral right of the author has been asserted

Set in 12.5/14.75 pt Monotype Garamond
Typeset by Rowland Phototypesetting Ltd, Bury St Edmunds, Suffolk
Printed in England by Clays Ltd, St Ives plc

ISBN: 978-0-141-03970-1

www.greenpenguin.co.uk

For Mary Imrie Hall, 1928–2008
And for my wife, Pamela

Contents

Foreword

'OPEN IT!' The voice was harsh and the old man flinched. He was used to giving the orders, not taking them.

Two stern-faced policemen stood either side of him, the dull metallic sheen of their handguns glinting in the tepid yellow light. They meant business and in the split second it took him to punch the six-digit code into the box which served as an electronic key, Josef Fritzl knew his rule of this macabre underworld had ended for ever.

A rumbling concrete door, something one of the policemen thought looked like a prop from an Indiana Jones movie, slid back and fetid, warm, musty air – ripe with the smell of mould, of sweat and of fear – washed past Fritzl and his unwanted guests. Fritzl was used to it, the policemen not. They gagged, reaching for handkerchiefs, sickened by the aroma. It seemed as if a corruption had occurred here and, now freed, it was leaching into their clothes and their skin, tainting them, embracing them, making them feel a part of the hideous conspiracy that had taken place within.

It was the early hours of Sunday, 27 April, 2008. The policemen had followed behind dungeon master Fritzl as he led them past seven locked doors, before the secret code had opened the eighth and final door to a hidden cavern, a dungeon where he had kept his own daughter as a sex slave for 24 long years. In this stinking, clandestine prison, he had fathered seven incestuous children with her, three of whom were brought up in the gloom for their entire lives; hunched, sallow-skinned, their gait uneven through lack of exercise, without a friend in the world save each other and their mother. Their courageous mother, Elisabeth, with whom – unlike other children – they had shared every single second of their lives.

A short while earlier, the last two dwellers of this underworld had been rescued and taken into care at a local clinic, where they had been reunited with their mother; Felix, 5, and Stefan, 18. Released into the arms of their grandmother on Friday evening after a lifetime hidden below her feet, they were pale and sick, distrustful and frightened, but also grateful – grateful beyond words, in any tongue – that they had escaped at last from their cement tomb.

The fact that only Elisabeth existed in official records, added to the appalling physical condition of the cellar dwellers, proved to police the story she had begun to relate was true. But even knowing the dungeon must exist, they could find no trace of it. The only hope for a quick solution was Fritzl himself. He was taken from his interrogation room at Amstetten police station and brought to the scene of his crime, leading the officers to his secret world, hidden behind a cupboard that was strewn with old paint tins, trays of nails and screws, discarded drill bits, wiring, rolls of insulating tape, brushes, transformers and plastic plant pots.

One later said that his first impression of what lay beyond the door, and his encounter just hours earlier with the inhabitants of this underground world, reminded him of a forced labour camp. During the Second World War there were two sub-camps of the Mauthausen-Gusen concentration camp in Amstetten, part of a complex where between 122,766 and 320,000 people died. The officer had seen pictures of slave labourers from the local gulag kept in appalling conditions, away from sunlight. But the war had finished 65 years ago and he never expected to see something like it on his beat. Things like this were part of history. Weren't they? Just what had happened here?

There could so easily have been other, more tragic endings. Kerstin, the desperately ill daughter who had been released from the cellar to get medical attention days earlier, and who was the catalyst for his downfall, could have died before Fritzl decided to let her go free. He could have stopped Elisabeth, the daughter he kept imprisoned as his personal breeding machine, from visiting her. But finally Fritzl the jailer – the controller, the supreme arbiter of light and darkness – had slipped up, and his grotesque tyranny was over. Within 24 hours the 23,000-strong population of the small Austrian town of Amstetten had swollen by nearly 1,000: these were the journalists and TV technicians who swarmed into the shell-shocked community to camp outside Fritzl's house and report on a saga of mind-numbing depravity.

There is a heroine in this tale of good and evil. Elisabeth, molested by her evil father and then forced to bring up the results of his uncontrollable urges, lavished love and attention on her six surviving children: a seventh who died in infancy was burned like he was so much rubbish in the heating incinerator of the house. Three lived with her, entombed, and never played with another child, never saw the stars or stood in the rain. Their entire existence was encased in a 55-square-metre windowless cellar carved out of the earth beneath the home of their jailer. In an even more bizarre twist, three children were allowed to live in the outside world – a world the cellar-dwellers knew simply as 'beyond the door' – unaware of the torment that their siblings and birth mother were undergoing every day beneath their feet, unheard and unknown.

This book examines the torture, the rapes, the suffering and the ultimate triumph of the human spirit when Elisabeth's anguished story was finally heard by a doctor. With her daughter dying, the spell was broken and she was able to relate a tale so diabolical it has no parallel in modern times. The world so far has seen an abstract picture of evil. In this book Fritzl the man – what motivated him, what pleased him, what warped him – is examined in detail. His complex finances are exposed alongside his equally complex sexual deviations. People who knew him, really knew him, as well as casual acquaintances, give revealing interviews.

Fritzl's earlier life is chronicled; the factors that led him to an adulthood of stunning cruelty. In these pages the reader will find a man who is more than the sum of his parts. That he is a monster is without question; but monsters live among us and wear human faces. The human face of Josef Fritzl represents the reverse of the coin, the side that must be scrutinized if a true portrait is to emerge alongside the monster portrayed in the media.

The same goes for Elisabeth, her father's magnificent

obsession. Here the friends from long ago paint portraits from memory of a girl they recall with fondness, even with love. Much of this book is devoted to her because her existence forged the destiny of Josef Fritzl. Friends, relatives, teachers and acquaintances have again gone out of their way to help tell her ghastly fate, her martyrdom at the hands of her own father.

Franz Polzer, the man who led the team which uncovered the cellar and its secrets, has given an exclusive interview about the whole macabre affair to this book. He details how Fritzl squirmed in the days before his secret was blown sky high, and bears testimony to Elisabeth's courage in the face of the extreme cruelty she endured. Herr Polzer is a man who expresses himself with precision, a man not given to hyperbole. He tells, in his own words, of a criminal case that was the simplest to solve and yet, at the same time, the most heartbreaking he will ever have to work on.

The final chapter of this book has yet to be written: Josef Fritzl must be declared either mad or bad. The former will ensure his captivity in a secure mental institution, the latter a trial and the certainty of years behind bars – for the remainder of his life, without question. Whatever his destiny, it will never be as grotesque as the one to which he sentenced his own daughter and his incestuous offspring.

Then there is the fate of the survivors, all scarred, physically and mentally, from the inhuman confinement they suffered. Therapy stretches ahead of them for years to come, aimed at easing them back into an alien world. But they are in a land without maps. As promising as their progress has been to date, no doctor can say with certainty how they will fare in the struggle ahead.

Finally, the Austrian nation must come to terms with what kind of society it is. The Amstetten case highlighted what appear to be grave flaws in the psyche of a people and its judicial and social structures, all of which failed Elisabeth and her children, as it failed another Austrian victim of underground confinement in 1998 – Natascha Kampusch, the girl in the cellar who endured an eight-and-a-half-year ordeal at the hands of her abductor. The land of Mozart and his music has proved itself deaf many times over in dealing with the ghosts of its Nazi past. Yet Josef Fritzl confessed that it was the spirit and the reality of those days which most influenced him, forged his character, made him what he was. If Nazi rule was the breeding ground for Fritzl's monstrous alter ego, then it is not unreasonable to suggest that its legacy made his countrymen the enablers of his elaborate crimes.

It has long been the Austrian habit to isolate un-pleasantness, controversy, to compartmentalize it and file it away out of sight while everyone gets back to the comforting images of snow-capped mountains and apple strudel – the wholesome, positive images of a modern European Union state. But those days are gone: Josef Fritzl has ensured that there must be a reckoning with both past and present for Austria. Its citizens can no longer lead lives based on *Schein nicht Sein* – the belief that how you seem is more important than how you really are. Fritzl's legacy must be the removal of this mindset; the victims of his 8,516-day reign of horror demand no less.

PART ONE
Master Plan

1. A Boy Called Josef

My programme for educating youth is hard. Weakness must
be hammered away. In my castles of the Teutonic Order a
youth will grow up before which the world will tremble. I
want a brutal, domineering, fearless, cruel youth. Youth must
be all that. It must bear pain. There must be nothing weak
and gentle about it. The free, splendid beast of prey must
once again flash from its eyes . . . That is how I will eradicate
thousands of years of human domestication . . . That is how
I will create the New Order.

Adolf Hitler, 1933

THE boy Josef was 26 days shy of his third birthday
when the Nazis came. Years later, he would tell his pals
at the Hauptschule Kirchengasse how he sat upon his
father's shoulders, his neck craned to watch them march
in, the bands playing, the banners waving in a soft spring-
time breeze. There was a carnival atmosphere as news of
Hitler's arrival in Austria spread, but Josef's father had
told his son the evening before of the serious importance
of the Germans arriving in his town. 'They have come
to save us, to save Austria,' he said. Josef didn't know
much about that but he liked their uniforms. He also

liked his father talking to him, something that didn't happen too often, unless he was being chastised.

Soon there was a throaty roar, partially drowning out the cheers of the crowd. Around the corner, a cumbersome G4 triple-axle open-topped Mercedes slowed down outside the discount department-store business of Adolf Greger, one of just a handful of Jews in the town who, along with his family, would later vanish and die on the orders of another Adolf, another Austrian, who now stood to give his trademark salute from the front passenger side of the massive vehicle. As it crawled through the main square the populace was dewy-eyed with admiration, hoarse from cheering, rosy-cheeked from beer, wine and natural exuberance. Adolf Hitler would soon become an honorary citizen of this small town; he would sign a letter to the mayor, saying how moved he was by the warmth of the welcome, although he expected nothing less.

Words like 'race', 'supermen', 'subhumans' were, not unnaturally, alien concepts for a kindergarten boy wearing lederhosen embroidered with edelweiss patterns. Yet these people marching in crisp columns, eyes ablaze with a purpose his nascent intelligence couldn't even guess at, had changed the starched, moodily reserved faces of his neighbours, turned them into smiling, laughing, jolly people. And that went for his father too. There were not many times in young Josef's life he could call his father 'jolly', so the day would leave an impression on him as big as a dinosaur's footprint in alluvial sand.

Josef waved his little paper swastika with his left hand, and raised his right in the favoured greeting of Austria's new rulers, when the grumbling motor car stopped yards from where he was perched.

'Sieg Heil!' they roared.

'Sieg Heil!' mimicked Josef.

Order, discipline, obedience. His father told him this was the trinity that inspired the brown-shirted tribe from beyond the border and, as much as a human being who has been alive for a little over 1,000 days can truly desire something, he fancied these were the role models for him. It was as if someone took a hypodermic syringe and injected the boy with the bacillus of extremism that would shape his DNA from this day forward.

Josef was witness to the German occupation of Austria, known as the 'Anschluss', or connection; an innocent term designed to mask the naked land-grab that subjugated the country to the Greater German Reich. Even its name disappeared – for the remainder of the Third Reich it was known as Ostmark – but its citizens were, for the most part, happy. Of course, the Jews had to vanish, but Austrian people didn't trouble themselves too much. During the Holocaust to come, Ostmark would supply 40 per cent of the staff and 75 per cent of the commandants of concentration and extermination camps. It was Austrians who, largely, organized the deportation of the Jews: 80 per cent of the people who worked for Adolf Eichmann, the supreme logistics planner for the mass murder, were from the land of mountains and meadows. Yet the ecstatic welcome that the Nazis received in Amstetten on 14 March, 1938, was replayed in towns and cities, hamlets and suburbs across the country during those heady times; only later would the country retreat into the comfortable, secure illusion that it was the first victim of its northern brothers. It was – and still is – a mental contortion which afforded the Austrian people much solace, but with often tragic consequences.

That night Josef's father took himself off to the bar at the Hotel Ginner as usual, the watering hole which would become the stamping ground for the Nazi elite during their stay in Austria. Order, discipline, obedience may have been abstract ideas that his father admired, but he cannot be said to ever have lived up to them. He was a bar-room worker and politician, someone who never put his beliefs into any sort of practice. Life was, for the most part, viewed through the bottom of an upturned lager glass. As he toasted the Nazis with his cronies, only child Josef was left with his mother, Maria. She was the strongest influence in his life, a woman of substance who, although bullied, did stand up to her wastrel partner whenever she could. The love once squandered on her husband was now channelled solely towards her son. He, in turn, adored her with a passion which, he would later confess, bordered on the obsessive.

Safe in the hometown he had seen transformed on this day, his mother bounced him on her knee and recited a favourite nursery rhyme, of the type beloved by children everywhere.

> This is the way the ladies ride,
> *Bounce, bounce, bounce.*
> This is the way the gentlemen ride,
> *Boom, boom, boom.*

> This is the way farmers ride,
> *Trot, trot, trot.*
> And this is the way the baby rides,
> *'Wheeee!'*

With that the giggling Josef was dropped carefully to the floor, to be gathered up seconds later in his mother's arms and smothered with love. It was the perfect end to a happy day.

It was also the beginning.

Josef Fritzl vowed never to be like his father – boozy, lazy, unreliable – but he was destined to copy him in many ways, as witnessed by his need to control, a compulsion to use his fists when his word no longer sufficed, and his relentless libido.

Fritzl's mother was married to a man called Karl Nenning in 1920, but he died in 1927, some eight years before Josef was born. She never married again, but she did have a lover, who was often not around. He was a cousin of Maria's, a drinker and a waster, and she threw him out for good four years after he fathered Josef. Having an illegitimate child in Catholic, archly-conservative rural Austria in those times was like having a scarlet letter daubed upon your front door. No attempt to cover up the child's illegitimate past could alleviate the shame that was visited on mother and boy by their neighbours, but – as Fritzl was to find in later life – memories are short and it is easy to rewrite the past.

At the time the Nazis came to town the boy Josef was destined to spend just one more year living with both mother and father in the family apartment. A man of poor character, restless, itinerant and unhappy in love, his father had already vanished once from his life. When Josef was born, his father was living in an adjoining town, working in a sawmill. But he came back shortly afterwards. They shared an apartment at Ybbsstrasse 40, a house that would later make the world hold its breath. Then, as in 2008, the house was divided up into individual apartments with tenants paying rent.

His father's presence contributed to a tense atmosphere in the household and family and friends say the young boy witnessed his mother being struck. He cannot have been unhappy when his father left for good when he was four; he was never to see him again. What became of Maria's lover is lost to history but, from now on, Josef was the little man of the household, an empty vessel waiting to be filled with all the attendant neuroses and problems that come with absentee fathers. He would display the symptoms to an astonishing degree later in life: heightened aggression, a feeling that he was 'special' and misunderstood, a need to be secretive, to control, to lie and manipulate – the departure of the father allowed these traits to nurture and grow within the boy. And all the while the mantra of order, discipline, obedience, as preached at the town kindergarten and reflected in daily life under Austria's new rulers, was seeping into his soul.

Josef hated his father, for his treatment both of him and his mother, but he wouldn't recognize that emotion until much later. He would remember the nights curled up in his cot with the blanket over his head to drown out the foul oaths his drunken father threw at Maria, and he would be eager to try to please him at breakfast the next morning with a cheery, 'Hello, Papa'. In some ways, given his industriousness, he was nothing like his father. But there is a saying in German: *Der Apfel fällt nicht weit vom Stamm.* The apple doesn't fall far from the trunk – or, like father like son. His genetic make-up could not divorce him from some of his father's more obnoxious traits – his lewd humour, his fondness for a beer, his infidelities, his utter need to control his wife, and the times he resorted to his fists when menacing and expletive-laced language was not enough to achieve the results he desired. These traits would hibernate until much later in a life destined to visit so much pain, fear and misery upon those whom he professed to love.

As a child in a town of fewer than 15,000 people, Josef was initially an oddity because he had no father; later, the demands of the war denuded most households of the male figurehead, but in those final years of peace, the family's situation was the butt of gossip and innuendo. At church on Sundays he felt the eyes of the other boys upon him, the eyes of the respectable housewives boring into his mother, silently condemning her for being unable to keep 'her man' at home. Theirs was to be a relationship of shared defiance against small-town opprobrium, an all-embracing overprotective love. Except that his mother often showed her affection with balled fists; she brought Josef up to respect the lash of the belt, the slap of the hand. Several neighbours from Josef's childhood days testify to the sternness of Maria. Yet Josef would always view his mother through rose-tinted spectacles. He described her as a 'character builder'; she was strict, she thrashed him when he didn't obey her, and she confined him to his room to do his homework. But, he said, she also wrapped him up in love, bonding with him at a deeper level than the love his schoolmates felt for their parents. All the while, in this inward-looking relationship, the seeds of future destruction were being sown.

With the Nazis as public role models – and his mother as a somewhat brutal role model at home – the boy Josef was slowly absorbing all the influences that would lie dormant within him until the day he could deny them no longer. Experts have shown that childhood environments which are emotionally unsupportive and characterized by poverty – lack of food, money, respect, social standing – are associated with sexual violence. Sexually aggressive behaviour in young men has also been linked to witnessing family violence, imprinted on Josef's young mind before his father abandoned the family.

To go some way to understanding Josef Fritzl later in life, it is necessary to comprehend the mother fixation he developed as a child. From his earliest days, and by his own admission, he felt a burgeoning love for his mother as he witnessed his father's coarse and violent behaviour towards her. Later, his feelings would morph into a need to denigrate women, to control them, to view them only as objects of lust, as things to be conquered, not loved, dominated, not respected. These feelings never left him.

Christine Riess (not her real surname) grew up in Linz and was destined to become Josef's sister-in-law. She describes Maria as 'a woman with an explosive temper, someone who resorted to violence against her son at the slightest infraction. Josef grew up without a father, and his mother raised him with her fists. That's about all you can say about it. She used to beat him black and blue almost every day. Something must have been broken in him because of that. He was unable to feel any kind of sympathy for other people. Yet he remained deeply, obsessively loving and loyal towards her.'

Hildegard Danielczyk was a neighbour for over 40 years and saw Josef growing up. She witnessed the relationship with his mother at first hand. She recalls: 'Fritzl was an only child and it was the gossip of the neighbourhood from the earliest days that his father had "gone away". Widowhood might have given the mother some more standing but, as it was, she was something of a pariah, having Josef out of wedlock. There was a very strong mother–son bond. She turned him out for school every day looking like he'd been polished, and he beamed with pride whenever he walked along beside her. But she also beat him fearfully.'

Official documents from the time that would shed more light on the affair have either been lost in the allied bombing of Amstetten or are covered by the cloak of Austrian data protection laws. But Frau Danielczyk recalls a problematic childhood that involved the young Fritzl being put into care on more than one occasion. She relates: 'I do not know the exact reasons, but I know that her son at this time kept being put into care. But he never stayed there very long. He was always escaping from the boys' home and going back home to his mother. Maria Nenning looked like a witch: she always wore a headscarf and big glasses, sometimes a straw hat. She was always dressed in dark clothes. All day long she was at home or in the garden. When the kids were playing too loudly she would look angrily out of the window and scream at them. She always looked upset with the world, was never friendly to the children in the neighbourhood. She was the kind of woman that people crossed the road to avoid. As a result, the boy was a loner with few friends to play with. It was a sad situation really.'

The hag analogy was taken up by another Ybbsstrasse resident, Werner Panowitz, who says: 'Fritzl's mother was a short, hunchbacked old woman who was weird, a bit like a witch. In former days all the local kids were afraid of her. She was known as "the piggy lady" because she looked dirty and dishevelled; her clothes were very shabby. The Fritzl family's background was quite modest.'

The Fritzl house may have taken in some money, but the widow Fritzl was not wealthy. It was old, bedraggled, shabby 'a real ramshackle hut', according to Peter Setz. With 28 years as a tenant there he was, aside from Josef, the longest resident. 'In my youth, it looked very different to how it looks today. There used to be four apartments inside, three of them consisting of two rooms. Only the Fritzl family apartment was bigger. My brother was the same age as Josef; he died last year. He knew him better than I did. I don't know what Maria and Josef lived on in those wartime days because the rents were very low because of the poor state of the property. The boy was obsessed with the mother and vice versa. She was a strange woman, shunned by others in the town who gossiped about her child being born out of wedlock. The boy clearly had complexes about who he was and what his standing was. He knew that tongues wagged –

had to. He knew he was different from the other kids.'

Josef Gatterbauer, 62, was a neighbour of Fritzl's in his youth, growing up in the house across the street. 'The person I have the most memories of is his mother,' he says. 'For us, he – Josef – was always known as Sepp Nenning. The house they were living in was widely known as the Nenning house. It was their property, but they rented out some of the rooms, so that there were always other families living under the roof. Mrs Nenning spent most of her time sitting on a bench that stood in front of our house. When I was a small boy we kids were often ordered to bring a piece of bread and water, and sometimes some apples as well, to give to the old woman out on the street. Sometimes she came into our house to give stuff to my parents because they ran a firm dealing with the transportation of goods, which was done with horses back then. She was a small and weird-looking woman. I remember her as the typical grandmother of those days. She lived with her son on money she got from the state – supplemented, I suppose, with the rent from the flats. I suspect things got easier for Josef as more and more lads lost their father in the war, and people had bigger things to worry about than illegitimacy. Having no father was not unusual when the bombs were falling.'

During the war Amstetten was not just an ordinary town. The young Josef was at the epicentre of a Nazi tyranny that included round-ups, beatings and murder. On 22 April, 1939, the Gestapo office in Linz reported to superiors in Berlin that political opponents had been rounded up and beaten, several needing hospitalization. The main square where Josef had been taken by his father to see the Nazis arrive was renamed Adolf Hitler Platz and the SS set up an office in town to coordinate the hunting down of Jews, gypsies, homosexuals, political rivals and myriad other state enemies in Amstetten and the surrounding communities.

The plan was to turn Amstetten into a model National Socialist community; before long the whole town resembled a Nazi advertisement with swastikas flying from every shop, the men dressed in a bedazzling array of party uniforms. Josef loved it. But 'order, discipline, obedience' translated into terror. At school, Josef Fritzl was taught, along with all the other children, to admire the might-is-right philosophy of the country's rulers, along with nourishing contempt for weakness and pity.

Throughout the war years Amstetten was home to a virtual foreign legion of slave labourers from all the conquered territories of the Reich: French POWs were put to work on the land; Hungarians repaired rail lines shattered by allied bombing; Russians cut down trees. The most pathetic victims of all were the inmates of the annexe of the terrible Mauthausen concentration camp. The pathetic, twisted wretches were seen by Josef, marching through town – on the way to work, or death.

What did these images mean to him? Was there any pity for them? Ironically, many years later, the tragedy would come full circle when the policemen who were about to destroy Josef Fritzl's strange and secret world would compare its inhabitants to the shocked survivors of a Second World War labour camp.

Josef was a month past 10 years old when the shooting finally stopped. Much of Amstetten had been reduced to smoking ruins, the streets gouged with bomb craters, the buildings blackened husks with all their windows shattered. Ybbsstrasse 40 survived, but the swastikas which had bedecked everything since 1938 – including Josef's family home – fluttered no more as all symbols of the Nazi state were forbidden.

The immediate post-war years were tough for Austria. Although the Soviets retreated from Lower Austria quite swiftly, making way for the British to move in as occupiers until 1955, Amstetten suffered like every other community from shortages of food, fuel, clothing and heating materials. There was an acute shortage of labour too: more than 50 per cent of Amstetten's menfolk who had marched off to fight for Hitler did not make it back home.

Karl Dunkl was a schoolmate of the young Fritzl for four years, from the age of 10 to 14. He recalls that Fritzl was two years older than the other boys in his class: 'This may have been something to do with the general turmoil in the aftermath of the war years, or the fact that he was bright but struggling; he had trouble at home, we all knew that. I think the mother had early dementia – she was certainly eccentric – and I think that, although she clobbered him, she really struggled to look after him. It was her inability to care, I think, that landed him in the children's home on a couple of occasions. Strange that his reaction was to run back home . . . He was an agitated boy, nervous, wary, seemed to have a bright, almost feral intelligence. He didn't like sitting still at all.'

Dunkl describes Fritzl as coming from a poor family

background. 'Poor in two aspects,' he recalls. 'One, because of the financial situation of the family, and two, because he was the only child of his mother he didn't have many social contacts. Fritzl was always solitary and pretty much a lone wolf. He played cowboys and Indians and cops and robbers with us in the woods, but being two years older he was a lot more physically advanced. He wasn't the leader, though; he seemed happier then being in the background.'

The boys often played football together in the streets – football was a passion that would stay with Fritzl throughout his life. But he wasn't very good at it; 'two-left-feet Fritzl' was one of the more polite insults hurled at him. He was also called a 'brauner' – from the brown shirts which the Nazis wore in the early days – as he continued to show youthful admiration for their policies. As a teenager Fritzl began to take an avid interest in his appearance and the opposite sex; twin pillars of his character that would define him for the rest of his life. Dunkl recalls: 'In the last two grades the age difference was more perceptible. Fritzl looked after his outward appearance meticulously and was always well groomed.'

Furthermore, Fritzl turned out to be one of the cleverer kids. He left school with a good academic record and spent five years studying electronic engineering, a much-needed skill in a country whose factories and workforce were both depleted. He was, by all accounts, a conscientious worker, a man with a meticulous eye for detail, one who never failed to gain adequate, and sometimes way above average, marks both for his practical and academic work. He had a two-hour return journey to college each day, and always shunned a drink with other students after classes to return home to his beloved mother.

At weekends, however, he began to shed some of his surliness and the traits of a loner that had defined his childhood. He became more relaxed, responded to the odd joke, even enjoyed telling a joke over a round of drinks, laughing with an infectious laugh as he joined in with his friends. He enjoyed a lively social life at weekends, going to dances in Amstetten or Linz, and later boasted of having had 'several girlfriends'. He liked girls and they liked him – he emulated the hairstyle of the American movie stars of the day and bought hair oil on the black market to slick it back. But he always returned at night to take care of his mother.

By the time he graduated from college he was 21, about to get his first job, and his character was formed. There would be forks in the road ahead and Josef Fritzl would have to decide which path to travel; but the combination of his fatherless upbringing, his maternal obsession, his compulsive need to assert authority and his wartime experience put him on autopilot towards a terrible destiny.

Leading Viennese psychotherapist Kurt Kletzer compiled a profile of Fritzl for this book, drawing on his formative years in Amstetten. Basing his analysis on Fritzl's background as described by peers, on his confession in 2008 and on the evidence of his crime, he concludes that his criminality was forged in his earliest days. 'What he experienced at the ages of two or three, possibly up to five, made him what he became later in life. The sexual fantasies he admits to having about his mother would have been grounded in the experiences he had as a very young child; it is no exaggeration to say that this is the stage when the inner soul of a person is created.

'Having an overly strict mother would have created tensions and pressures that his still-forming mind would not be able to cope with, not be able to process in a logical fashion. Clearly, the society of the times – strict, censorious, brooking no dissent – would have allowed for no outlet from these pressures. He was a young volcano ready to blow. It would have warped him because such feelings of frustration need somewhere to go.

'These frustrations would have been manifold: the feeling of being different from his peers because he doesn't have a dad; the feeling of impotence because his mother doesn't reward his devotion; a skewed idea of what is good behaviour, and what punishment is acceptable for crossing the line. Somebody like Fritzl who starts out in life as a victim, with a strict mother and a father who is no longer around, is perpetually asking himself, "Why me?" They perversely enjoy, in some ways, regarding themselves as a victim, and we all know that all too often the victim later becomes the perpetrator.

'All the time he was growing up he needed to empty the hate in his heart, but he could never quite open the valve. Instead of a way out he built the foundations of his personality at this stage, which made him what he was – creating the man who later went on to become a rapist and a multiple sex offender.'

A few short years later Josef Fritzl would become 'known to the police' – a phrase that is barely adequate to describe the man who perpetrated a string of sex offences, the brutality of which would devastate the lives of at least two young women.

2. The Evil Within

The man had watched the house for nights on end. Casually strolling past, sometimes riding on his bicycle. He noted when the man left to go to work, saw when the lights went on and off, plotted his strategy accordingly. Always plan things: that was the Fritzl way. On the night he chose to strike the weather was fine – a low moon, a light breeze, a clear sky. He felt the knife in his pocket, liked the antiseptic feel of the clean, cool blade. He felt the usual stirrings, the beast that could not be denied. Oh, he was going to enjoy this one, all right. Moving stealthily across the street he came to the window, forced it open and was inside within seconds. Creeping noiselessly into the bedroom he pounced on the young occupant in her negligee, produced the knife and came to take what he regarded as rightfully his.

Fritzl the confused boy entered the world of work at the age of 21 when he got a job with the Voestalpine steel company in Linz. It was 1956 and Austria, like Germany, could not produce material quickly enough for the rebuilding of destroyed cities, the reconstruction of the shattered wartime economy. Work was to be had everywhere, the result of a depleted manpower pool lost in battle, captured or simply expelled; many skilled Jewish workers were among those lost when Austria fell under the rule of Nazi Germany. Fritzl liked the masculine camaraderie of his new workplace, enjoyed the feeling of being a man among men as he toiled on complex electronic machinery in the steel rolling mills, journeying home each evening, as usual, back to the bosom of his mother.

And then, the following year, aged 22, he met Rosemarie. She was 17 and the perfect wife for an apprentice monster. She did what she was told, she could cook, she could clean, she didn't have much to say for herself and, to parody an old saying, when he wanted her opinion, he would give it to her. As Rosemarie's former best friend Elfriede Hoera said in an interview for this book: 'He viewed her as a farmer views a prize cow: she was someone who would give him what he wanted – namely, a large family – and he demanded she respect his need for utter subservience in the relationship. I could never understand the two Rosemaries, the one free from him who was caring, funny and loving, and the withdrawn, subservient and silent person she became on the rare occasions they were together. By the time I met her she was totally under his control, but I believe they'd been like that since she first met him. Even her parents, whom I know she loved, hadn't liked him, although I didn't then know why, but it made no difference. He had total control over her.'

At first Rosemarie's parents had been delighted at the match, just like their daughter. They were pleased when he came to stay with them at their home in Linz – he was working for Voest, which was just down the road, and they welcomed him into their home warmly. Rosemarie was timid at first, awed by the handsome, tall, muscular boy; it was only later that she would grow to fear him, as all those in his orbit feared him. Born on 23 September, 1939, and raised in Linz, Rosemarie was a typical girl of the time whose ambitions stretched no further than the three K's of Austrian female society at the time – *Kinder, Küche, Kirche*, or children, cookery, religion. She had completed a course as a kitchen assistant, which would qualify her to work in any one of the pubs and restaurants in town, but she had little else in the way of prospects, looks or confidence. 'Josef was everything to her,' said Elfriede. 'She felt she was destined for the shelf until he came along.'

They met at a dance in Linz early in the year and married in the summer. He promised her he would be rich, that he had a home already in his mother's house, that he would be a good provider and a faithful husband. The lies started from the beginning; they would continue for 51 pain-filled years.

Just as the Nazis he admired made their subjects feel better about themselves by thinking the worst of others – in their case, the Jews – Fritzl bolstered his ego by putting Rosemarie down from the start. She was lazy, she was slovenly, she was getting fat, she was getting dowdy; her sister Christine said the insults were never-ending and all aimed at putting himself above her. She was a classic study in abuse – a woman who suffered in silence, as her daughter would later suffer, as all her children, in one way or another, suffered.

Three years later the most important woman in his life died. It was 1959 and Maria Nenning passed on. Associates from the time say Fritzl was 'gutted' by her death and wore a black armband for a month. He may have been married but his heart still belonged to his mother. It is interesting to note that the year she died was the year he first came to the notice of police in Linz for exhibitionism; it was as if her influence had previously kept him in check.

It is a conundrum for doctors piecing together the puzzle of Josef Fritzl that he wanted a large family. His was a rare kind of narcissism, a total and relentless need for his own needs to be satisfied above everything else. A family meant responsibilities and costs, time and energy. Yet the ideal of a large brood was an integral part of the Fritzl master plan; it was what he had dreamed of, growing up as an only child. And Rosemarie would not disappoint him on that score, producing seven children over the years – Ulrike in 1957, Rosemarie in 1960, Harald in 1963, Elisabeth in 1966, twins Gabriele and Josef in 1971 and Doris in 1972.

'Rosemarie was a slip of a girl when they met and married and she produced children for him pretty soon afterwards,' recalls neighbour Frau Danielczyk. 'She wasn't a beauty but she was nice; the kind of woman, I suppose, mothers like their sons to marry, although I don't expect Mrs Nenning would have been all that pleased. He was her world; I'm sure she saw Rosemarie as an interloper. God knows what conversations they had when he took her home. But Rosemarie's mother and father were not in favour of him towards the end, and after the trouble – I mean, he had four children with her when, you know, he went inside . . .'

*

Police profiling experts recognize there are four kinds of rapists out there: the power-assertive rapist, the anger-retaliation rapist, the power-reassurance rapist and the anger-excitation rapist. Experts believe Fritzl falls into category three because these rapists lack the self-confidence and interpersonal skills to develop proper, meaningful relationships with women. Women are to be conquered, subdued, the way a mountaineer conquers a peak or a matador slays a bull. The FBI rule book states:

```
He lives or works near his victim, and
pre-selects her by peeping or stalking.
He typically breaks into her home in the
early hours of the morning and awakens
her. He uses minimal force and will
threaten her with a weapon, but sometimes
does not have one. He fantasizes that he
is his victim's lover, so he may ask her
to disrobe or to wear a negligee, and he
will kiss her and engage in foreplay. The
power-reassurance type accounts for 21 per
cent of rapists. He is the least violent
type of rapist, and does not intend to
hurt or kill you. Among the different
types of rapists, he is most likely to
be dissuaded if you scream, cry, plead
or fight.
```

In 1967, at the age of 32, married, with children, with prospects and in full possession of his faculties, Josef Fritzl laid the foundation stone of the dungeon in which he would later imprison his daughter Elisabeth. Working in Linz, he began to monitor the home of a nurse whose husband worked nights. One night he decided to strike, his libido overriding the normal circuits of a man who had much to lose. He climbed through a window, entered the bedroom, brandished a knife and held it to his victim's throat. Power coursed through him; he loved it.

The lady is 65 now. She would never see Josef Fritzl again in the flesh, but she saw him all right, during those mad days of April 2008 when his face became a global symbol for evil. She saw those eyes and the healing process of 41 years evaporated. 'As soon as I saw his picture on TV, I knew it was him. I recognized him by the eyes. I couldn't sleep the whole night after that,' she said. 'It was as if what he did to me happened yesterday. I remember someone pulling the bedclothes back, and I thought it was my husband coming home,' she went on. 'But then I felt this knife being pushed against my throat. He told me: "If you make a noise I'll kill you." Then he raped me.'

Experts who have to deal with such attackers and their victims believe he wouldn't have killed her, but she was not to know that. Retired Linz police chief Gerhard Marwan described Fritzl's rape of the nurse as 'a brutal attack'. He led the team which caught Fritzl, and explained: 'We traced him by a print from his palm at the scene, and he was identified by the victim as well.'

Fritzl was driven by a berserk sex drive coupled to an astonishing self-belief that he was taking what was owed to him. The fantasies he had of sexual contact with his mother had nourished him during his formative years;

now, no woman could match up to the memory of Maria. He viewed women as objects to satisfy him, fit for one thing only. They were all bitches, whores, sluts. As the working girls in the local brothels would later testify, he treated women as devoid of human feelings, therefore unworthy of tenderness or respect.

But the nurse in Linz was not the first; one month earlier he had attempted to rape a 21-year-old woman. According to a file held by the police, Fritzl dragged her into the Ebelsbergerwald woods. She managed to escape and later identified him as her assailant. The file also details his record for 'exhibitionism', flashing in the local woods to lonely hikers – another manifestation of his power complex, his total disregard for women as human beings.

Since his arrest in 2008, another woman has come forward to claim she was also raped by Fritzl in the late 1960s. The victim, who was 20 at the time, said the rapist climbed through her bedroom window: 'I felt this knife being pushed against my throat. He told me: "If you make a noise I'll kill you."' These were the exact same words he said to the nurse in Linz. 'Then he raped me. I was too embarrassed to report it to the police. I am one hundred per cent sure that it was Fritzl.'

Ultimately, it was the rape of the nurse for which he was convicted and sentenced to 18 months in jail. The judge who handed down his punishment said it would have been longer 'had you not been a man of previous good character with a wife and four children'. Fritzl served less than one year for his crime, his earlier crimes unreported and unpunished. The Austrian judicial system would see to it that his criminal record would be erased by the time he came around to putting the finishing touches to his master plan.

Fritzl lost his job as a result of his spell in jail, and earned the undying suspicion of his in-laws. 'I was 16 at the time and I found the offence simply disgusting – all the more so seeing as he already had four children with my sister,' said Rosemarie's sister Christine. His wife, by now cowed and used to his abominable ways, masked her pain by choosing to believe the police had arrested the wrong man. Those who know her say it was the only way she could live with herself – and him. It was the start of Rosemarie's denial of the obvious – that her husband was a monster – and her creation of an alternative reality that would come crashing down around her in April 2008.

Frau Danielczyk witnessed the transformation: 'She became, in time, terrified of him. I asked once why she didn't leave him; she told me it would be madness to do that. She said he was "mad and violent" and that she was certain he would "shoot me" if she ever tried to get a divorce. She was always terrified of losing the children. Of course it went around the neighbourhood like wildfire that he was away serving time and that it was for rape. Rosemarie was terrified that if she made a move to go she would lose the children. And after a while into that marriage, they were all she lived for. After all, he was a respected businessman and engineer and she was, as she told me, "an uneducated housewife". I know that Rosemarie's parents weren't in favour of her staying with Fritzl after the rape. I once spoke to her mother about it, and she told me how unhappy she was with her daughter's marriage, but there was nothing she could do. She knew that Rosemarie was too afraid to leave Fritzl and she just had to grin and bear it. Her father wasn't happy either, but there was little he could do. He was blind by that time. He didn't really have a lot of opportunity to help his daughter to leave her unhappy marriage. What sustained Rosemarie was this great love for her children.'

Rosemarie told the children that their papa had 'gone abroad' to work when he was arrested, but they would doubtless have heard neighbourhood rumours. Regardless, they never questioned him; the tyranny, the demand for respect and obedience, dominated their lives from the day they were born.

Austria was, and remains, a deeply conservative society and a man with a record as a sexual predator would have been fortunate to get a second chance. But it was Fritzl's good fortune that the desperate shortage of manpower, and in particular of qualified people, meant he was not idle for long. When he was released from jail he went on holiday to put some distance between him and his crime, and he first met the man who was to become his lifelong friend, Paul Hoera. With his love of Germany Fritzl discovered a friend in Hoera; their children were of the same age, they shared a mutual love of football and Rosemarie's cooking, and with his former friends probably only too aware of his criminal past, he started to reinvent himself as a hardworking engineer and a loving but strict father. At the same time, he set out to erase the past that he had created.

On his return to Amstetten he quickly landed a job

with a firm that was desperate for people of his talents and prepared to look away if Fritzl's past was not all they could have desired. He landed a job with Zehetner Baustoffhandel und Betonwerk GmbH, a building materials company in Amstetten, where he worked from May 1969 until December 1971. His speciality was in concrete extrusion devices and making machines for what was then an extremely specialized job. 'He was hired even though he had a record,' said Sigrid Reisinger, whose father took him on. 'I know the crime was of a sexual nature but I don't recall the precise details. My father knew what he had done of course, but like so many people he was taken in. He once told me that Fritzl was a genius at finding solutions to engineering problems; he would be given a problem and would tackle it like others would approach a game of chess. It was a challenge, and he didn't give up until he had a winning strategy. Once he had spent a bit of time at the firm – and I recall it was a shaky start because there were people who certainly didn't want him there, such as my mother – at the end of the day he quickly became indispensable. All my mother could do was make sure we kept away from him; she knew what he had done and never trusted him. However, those were difficult times and the bottom line was that he was very good at what he did, and he was quickly in a position where the firm couldn't manage without him.'

The revelations about Fritzl also came as no surprise to another former member of the Zehetner team. 'I wouldn't put it past him,' says Franz Haider, who shared a desk with Fritzl. 'This is in hindsight of course. It must be. But he had an explosive temper that was allied to a true genius at what he did. So if someone was going to do what he went on to do, I guess I would say the cap fitted him.

'We worked together developing a machine to cast concrete pipes used in sewers – underground again, eh? It was a big machine, very complex, five metres high and three metres wide. He was appointed technical director here and was working on the project for months; it was his pride and joy and he was determined to get it right. I was his assistant and, as such, spent a lot of time with him. You would think that being together a lot would have revealed much about him, but I learned nothing except that he was married. He kept everything to himself. He didn't take or make any private phone calls at work. There were no family pictures on his desk, no small talk about what the kids got up to, or about what his interests were. I say this because, looking back, he was obviously a man who could compartmentalize things; he didn't need to share. And so, if anyone was capable of keeping a monstrous secret, something hidden under his house, then I would say he would be the ideal candidate. Fritzl's area of speciality was concrete; he knew everything about the material and the technology that related to it. He was a genius with it. As the world came to know, right?'

After his spell at the materials firm he was on the road for two years as a salesman with the Rimes machinery company, based in Germany. Police on the Fritzl case in 2008 have asked to examine force archives of cold cases across Germany and Austria to see if there are unsolved sex crimes that occurred at the time he was in the vicinity. They are matching up his expenses and appointments with crime reports in numerous locations. Painstaking, plodding work, but work which might prove that his sexual hunger was truly insatiable.

From 1973 until 1996 Fritzl and his wife owned the guest house 'Seestern' – Lake Star – and also a campsite at Unterach am Mondsee, some 140 or so kilometres from Amstetten. Acquaintances say this was a decision that seems, for once, to have been taken jointly in their marriage. Fritzl was keen to be more self-reliant, no longer a 'wage slave', as he told his friend Hoera. The opportunity to escape a workplace where his past was well known was also on his mind. Rosemarie, for her part, had worked in pubs and restaurants as a teenager and knew something of the trade.

Fritzl met a new circle of pals centred on Hoera. Both had a dislike of authority and were constantly looking for get-rich-quick schemes. Slowly others who had rented plots of land to locate static caravans in the area joined their social circle. One Austrian, Herbert Herbst, recalls: 'The children would play among themselves. All of us seemed to have kids, although Rosemarie's kids had a lot of work to do in the guest house. We would all sit by the shore, in each other's gardens, or at the local restaurants. They were good times – but none of us had any idea of Fritzl's past.'

Hoera recalls the Mondsee purchase was the first business deal he saw his friend engage in, one that took him from owning a small apartment house to controlling a multimillion-pound property empire. He says: 'The guy who owned the land didn't really want to spend all the cash on developing it properly, and it really needed investment.

It was a beautiful spot, right alongside the lake, with the road at the back of the field and the guest house nearby. But there was only one electricity plug for the whole place; in summer there were so many extension plugs in it that it looked like a cactus, and then there was a flagpole in the middle advertising the place, and that was it.

'He bought it from a guy called Michael Werner ... Fritzl got it at a knock-down price because there had been trouble flogging it before. They signed the deal at the lawyer's and Fritzl said he thought Werner's eyes were going to pop out when he paid for the property in full – in cash – just like that. Werner stuck a brick wall up on one side of the property, which blocked all the doors to the lake, and so Fritzl put an open cesspit in front of Werner's front door. They hated each other after that. The cesspit would flood during rainstorms and the effluent would go into the lake. They were always fighting each other or threatening legal action over something.'

To cement his position in the local community, Fritzl set about getting the campsite and guest house into shape. A guest from the time recalls the first thing that went up was a huge sign: 'Guest house Seestern. Owner: Engineer and Hon. Consulate Josef Fritzl'. Although she had little choice in the decision to take over the property, those who knew Rosemarie said she loved the chance to be away from her domineering husband – despite the hard work and the fact that, inevitably, some of the time there was spent away from her beloved children. She built up a group of loyal regulars, people who would either come every year for a three-week holiday, or others who stationed a caravan at the campsite all year round.

Herbst remembers: 'There were a lot of us who'd been coming here for years. What more could you want? Good friends, with Rosemarie's great food. It was cheap – and the scenery is magnificent. Rosemarie was really good on the traditional Austrian stuff, which is of course what we all came for – schnitzel, apple strudel, cheese dumplings and sauerkraut.

'Her old man wasn't there that often. He was a bit of a weird one, not a typical guest-house owner. I mean, he would never buy drinks for the regulars and, if the work-load got heavy, you wouldn't see him getting up to help serve the drinks, or help in the kitchen. And although there were plenty of rooms, they were for guests. He made sure his family slept in an old caravan they kept on the field nearby. He could tell a joke all right, though, and he was interesting to talk to – but it was always mostly practical stuff. He wouldn't sit there talking about his life, unless it was work.

'At the time I saw him most he was on a lot of foreign assignments. He spent a lot of time in India building bridges, he said, and he was in South America as well. We didn't really miss him when he wasn't around. Rosemarie changed when he was there. She was always happiest when the kids were there – and most miserable when he was around. She arrived in May and shut up in September, so that meant the kids had May and June with old Fritzl in Amstetten, then they would come and join her later for their summer holiday, in July and August. She really missed them.

'But, as I said, she was a joker. I sometimes used to invite all the people from our group and their kids –

might have been a few dozen at its peak – to my plot for a barbecue, and she would come and shout, "Herbst, you've stolen all my customers again!" But she was only joking – every time we went there for a schnapps afterwards, the place was always packed. Her cooking was really famous.

'I know the kids all had to help her. They were all really nice – apart from the son Sepp, who was a bit of a loner, impossible to talk to. Rosemarie was the beauty, all the boys liked her, and Elisabeth, she was the shy one, but good for babysitting. And then of course she joined the sect – or so we thought.'

Paul Hoera recalls that Fritzl and his wife never let slip any inkling of his past in their time there: 'Josef knew the Mondsee because he first took his kids there on holiday in 1969; must have been just after his bit of trouble. His children were playing with mine and he came to collect them. I remember thinking how tightly wound he was. "Get back home, NOW!" he shouted at them. I told him that he should take it easy, come and sit with me and we could drink a beer together. I found out later that he didn't usually have much to do with Austrians and seemed to like the Germans much more, and because I was a German he agreed to stay for that beer.

'That was how our friendship started. I remember at the Mondsee later, when he had the guest house, he used to go fishing a lot with his sons Harry and Sepp (Josef). Sepp was his favourite, you could tell. The girls never went on any fishing jaunts; he told me they had to stay behind and help Rosemarie with "women's work". They had to make the beds and clean the rooms. I remember my daughter used to go and help the girls as well, so that they could finish earlier and they could go off and have fun together. My daughter was never paid, she did it just to help her pal. I don't think he ever knew they used to sneak off earlier than planned.

'Fritzl was a mass of contradictions – clearly a tartar to his kids but engaging as a bloke. He liked the odd beer but wasn't a real drinker. He had a hearty laugh. He liked to watch Tom and Jerry cartoons on the telly and guffaw like a toddler. We started to take some trips away together. We went to the Oktoberfest in Munich but he didn't get sozzled – just a couple of beers, some chicken or some roasted pork knuckle. He seemed to like being among the crowd, got a buzz out of seeing people enjoy themselves.

'But he was also a very vain man, liked to keep trim, get a tan. He was going bald very quickly and one time, when I hadn't seen him for a few weeks, we met up and I noticed that he had more of a thatch than before. I thought it was a wig but he said he had been to Sweden to get a transplant. The next time we went to Munich together for a lads' weekend. I had to traipse around with him to a clinic so he could get hold of some special cream he had to slather on his head to stop the new hair from falling out. It was a good 20 years ago and he paid 400 marks a time for it then. I have heard him since described as stingy – and he was, in many ways, except on himself.'

Elfriede Hoera, Paul's ex-wife, lives alone in a small flat in Munich, far away from the stifling provinciality of Amstetten. She recalls: 'We had two sons and a daughter. The sons were around the same age as Josef's older daughters, while my youngest was about the same age as

Elisabeth. I had very little to do with Josef. He was more Pauli's friend – he was a big man, I remember. I spent more time with Rosemarie. She was great to talk to, but only after work and when he wasn't around. I used to help her get the work behind her so we could enjoy some time together. She was just a workhorse to her husband. She always did the cooking, ironing, washing, cleaned the rooms, swept the floors, did the books. The children were recruited on lots of occasions and I pitched in to help so she could get done quicker and we could have some tea or coffee together.

'Rosemarie always had to do what he wanted. He was always friendly to me, although I never knew about his past. If I had known about his rape conviction it would have totally changed my opinion. I certainly would have paid more attention to his relationship with my children and his. But we never knew. He was friendly with my daughter and the other children, and made jokes. He was a funny man when he wanted to be. At least, with other people. After Paul and I divorced I didn't have any-thing to do with him. Or with Rosemarie. I think because Josef would have taken Paul's side – he wouldn't have liked her being friends with me any more – and in any case she always made it clear that the one important thing in her life was the children. Everything else was secondary to her.

'He was a dictator at home. He ruled everybody with an iron fist. That included his wife. But she was completely trapped, in that she had seven children with him and they were everything to her. She couldn't leave them; it wasn't possible for her to even consider it. So she just got on with it. I'm positive she knew nothing about what was going on with Elisabeth. But who would have thought that someone could do something like that? Especially your own husband. Your own daughter. She also had enough work looking after the children and with the business to keep her occupied. She didn't have a lot of time for reflecting on her own life and how she might want to change things. If she had, things might have changed. As it was, she was just a workhorse. I never once saw her in anything other than work clothes at Mondsee and when I remarked on it within earshot of Josef, he said, "She doesn't need a cocktail dress to cook dinner in." She never wore much make-up when he was around and it was absolutely forbidden for the girls to use any, but they always put some slap on when he wasn't around. That's just part of growing up, but he couldn't see it like that. It was always his way or the highway.

'On special occasions, such as Christmas or Easter, Rosemarie would be cooking and he would be in control of the conversation, as always. Every time, and I mean every time, when the family was together, the atmosphere was strange and stilted with an underlying air of menace pervading everything. The children were living in fear and, if they happened to be doing something when he wasn't around, they would instantly stop and pretend they had been up to nothing at all. It was a hell of a life for them.'

Helmut Greifeneder is the former head of the administrative authority that covers Mondsee. When speaking of Fritzl, he recalls: 'He wasn't a sociable type. Not unfriendly to deal with on an official level, but you wouldn't

want him down the tennis club or the pub. He had his little
projects and that was what he stuck to. He was known
for not wanting to spend money, but he wasn't a stupid
man. I don't think anyone ever underestimated him.

'On one occasion we told locals renting out their fields
to campers that they had to install drainage facilities for
toilets and washrooms. It was because of the overflowing
drains and complaints from campers – you can't have
sewage going straight into the lake if you want people
to swim in it. But Fritzl and several others were up in
arms, although it was their own fault. He sent threatening
letters, talking about going to court. But with him, he
only pushed it so far – when it finally came to the court
date, and it was a question of put your money where your
mouth is, he backed down – he didn't want to spend
money on lawyers, and he knew he would lose. I think
his fellow landowners were a bit let down by that. He left
them in the lurch. It only made the row between him and
Werner worse.

'I think it worked like this: the wife, Rosemarie, was
here from May to September when the season was in full
swing; he was back in Amstetten with the children in May
and June because they were still at school. He took the
children back home a month before Rosemarie joined
them to restart school. Rosemarie worked hard here, there
was always lots to do. I can't imagine that Fritzl ever got his
hands dirty. He never worked as a waiter or helped out in
the house or made the beds or cleaned the kitchen. I have
checked the records: they show that the entire business was
in her name, but of course that doesn't mean she had any
power or a say in how it was run. I guess he did it for tax

reasons, like a lot of other people. And of course, if there were to be problems arising over debts, then they couldn't take it off him because it was in her name.

'His was a very dominating personality. What he said went. The conversations I had with him regarding planning matters showed he knew exactly what he wanted and how to get it. But he absolutely was not a likeable man. I couldn't possibly judge how Fritzl treated his wife and kids when there was nobody around. But his wife was very reserved, to us it almost seemed like she was a slave to him.'

The Mondsee years provided a distraction from routine for the children, and they enjoyed life when their father was absent in Amstetten, pursuing new business deals. But when he was with them the bucolic country idyll was just another setting for their misery.

It was also a place where his agile criminal mind rehearsed future events. Many years later, with his finances verging on ruin, strange fires would break out at the Ybbsstrasse flat. The training for these, it seems, happened at the guest house. Barely a year after it was purchased, a fire broke out in broad daylight; a passing policeman stopped and helped an exasperated Fritzl stamp it out. Just a carpet and an old Formica-topped cabinet were damaged and Fritzl muttered something to the officer about the electrics. The policeman was not so certain but, with no one injured, he didn't report it. In 1982 there was another blaze, this time more serious, which consumed most of the back of the wooden guest house. This time police did investigate and concluded it had been caused by a gas bottle deliberately placed near an open flame. Fritzl was suspect number one.

Hoera explains: 'I only found out when he called me to tell me. He said: "Guess what, Pauli? They think I burned the house down!" It was only later that I found out how serious it was, and that they were going to arrest him. I thought it was great fun and made a big joke about it, and every time I saw him I'd shout out: "Look out everyone, here comes the arsonist!" But he didn't find it very funny. He would be quite grumpy about it. If we'd known then that he had previous convictions for sex offences, we would never have had anything to do with him. But we never knew. He hid everything. He was great at covering up what he didn't want you to know, it seems. A lot of people talk about how he was always a dark horse. He was.'

But a court in Wels that had to sanction further investigation ordered the probe dropped because of lack of 'substantial evidence'. With no criminal proceedings against him, his insurance company had no alternative but to pay up. With a considerable sum in compensation (the equivalent of over £50,000) Fritzl was able to build a much larger guest house and handed the day-to-day running over to Rosemarie while he concentrated on his latest scheme; real estate.

He was fascinated – as he told Adolf Graf, the man from whom he rented some land around the guest house – by the concept of 'money earning money'. Graf recalls: 'He fancied himself as a real-estate magnate, thought he would be good at it. I don't know about that – I only have memories of the way he behaved and I wasn't all that impressed. He was clearly the lord of the manor. Even at his campsite, he was very strict and his rules had to be followed. I remember him as a man of no flexibility whatsoever, and of no sensitivity either. If you were sick, or something happened, he didn't care ... there was a rule and that was it. He was tyrannical when it came to work. He expected a lot from others, but he seemed to expect a lot from himself too. Saturdays, Sundays, holidays – if work needed to be done, he did it.'

One conversation that Hoera recalls now is chilling when he thinks of all that came to pass. 'On the campsite we had an important police inspector from Salzburg. Over a beer or two with me and Josef he told us the story of an Austrian man who was banged up in a police cell for being drunk. He said that the cops forgot he was there – just like that, literally forgot – and the guy died of thirst. "Really?" asked Josef. "He was underground and you couldn't hear him, not hear him at all?" The police-man said no. "That's very interesting," added Josef and, as he said it, he had a look on his face he didn't usually have. He was never one for small talk but he really seemed to drink all the details in. "How can someone forget that they put someone in the ground, forget all about them like that? It's beyond belief, isn't it?" I told him that everyone gets swallowed up by the earth eventually. He said, "I suppose they do, Paul, I suppose they do."'

Hoera thinks this conversation took place sometime in the late 1970s – the time when Fritzl was formulating his master plan for his own place under the ground, a plan that would utilize all his cunning and all his skills with machinery and concrete.

Around this time Fritzl also began collecting books on the Nazi era, biographies of the party bigwigs like Albert Speer, Heinrich Himmler, Josef Goebbels, Martin Bormann and Hermann Goering. He spent money on videos from America that were unobtainable in Austria or Germany, and brushed up on the English he had learned in school so that he could understand them. Here were a group of men he could really relate to: people who took what they wanted, and damn the consequences. He assembled a literary shrine to the Third Reich that would be discovered by the police many years later.

With money in his pocket and the memory of the rape conviction receding, he decided it was time to see a bit of the world. The cellar idea was forming, but had not yet crystallized when he and Hoera hit on the idea of a holiday in Thailand. The sexual revolution had not reached Amstetten by the time he and Hoera were drinking mile-high gin and tonics en route to Bangkok; but the reputation for easy sex that the country offered was well known. To a man who had turned away from his wife, it seemed to be a paradise well worth visiting.

'I suggested to him that we go there and he bit my arm off,' says Hoera. ' "It's sex on tap there, isn't it?" I laughed, thought he was joking. I actually wanted to go there to de-stress a bit. I had been once before, on my own, and loved it but thought I would like a bit of male company next time. Personally, I avoided the sex clubs. I don't think they were the cleanest joints in the world. I left the girls alone. When I got there with Josef in 1977 we stayed for nearly four weeks. We shared a room together, it was really cheap.

'He spoke English really quite well, which helped a lot in Thailand because not many people spoke German. He fitted in immediately. He prepared himself before he went, reading up books on Thai food, customs, that sort of thing. On the first day he went off for a massage – I don't know if he went for the "extras", that would have been too much information for me. It set the pace of the holiday; he had one every day after breakfast, said it set him up. He got into hot, fiery food, long drinks and he went clubbing. I'm pretty sure he went whoring, but not with me. In the last week he stuffed his suitcase with a massive number of cheap T-shirts and collected a number of cheap suits that he was measured for by an Indian tailor at the start of the holiday. They were nice suits, looked expensive, but they were as cheap as chips really.'

When on this, their first jaunt abroad, Hoera never saw Fritzl write a postcard to his family. He can't recall him phoning home, or even mentioning them at all. It was a dry run for longer periods abroad when there was to be much more at stake than the takings of the guest house to worry about.

It is apparent that the Mondsee years were used by Fritzl to put distance not just between himself and his crimes, but also between himself and Rosemarie – both physically and spiritually. She spent long periods at Mondsee, either alone or with the children, while he pursued his own unique timetable. Abused, shunned, unloved, belittled and betrayed, her capacity for sacrifice – 'everything for the children' – turned her into his unwitting chief accomplice.

Rosemarie's former colleague Anton Klammer says:

'People ask how she could not have known, but she was living away from him for a long time. Josef beat her and she was petrified of him. She loved her kids but the guest house they owned was a good excuse to be apart from him and to have a little peace. Rosemarie was a happy and normal person, but when he was around she used to shrink away. You could tell she was terrified of him.'

Yet her absence was the biggest factor in enabling Fritzl to carry out his master plan. Many nights he was alone in Ybbsstrasse, plotting the surreptitious jail, left undisturbed by anyone. In Rosemarie he had created the perfect assistant: a frail, cowardly thing, tormented by his rages but unable to free herself from his thrall. When the terrible secret of the hidden dungeon was finally revealed, there were many headlines which questioned how she could not have known about what occurred just metres beneath her feet. There was suspicion that she was somehow involved in a macabre folie à deux – a madness shared by both husband and wife. The police knew better: Rosemarie was a victim long before Elisabeth became one. She was a victim when she took that first dance with Fritzl, shared that first kiss with him, shared his bed with him. She was plunged head first into the nightmare because she simply did not know such evil could exist.

But it existed all right, its dark heart beating next to hers on the few occasions – the very few – when they shared a bed together. 'He had contempt for her, ultimately,' explains Kletzer, the psychoanalyst. 'He has a psychopathic need to control her and, in controlling her, maps out the groundwork for even more diabolical behaviour. Any challenge or objection by his wife is met with rage, temper tantrums, or stony silence. If she changes a particular behaviour to please him, another behaviour becomes the target of his anger. The definition of what pleases him constantly changes, so that she is kept off balance.

'He assumed from day one he had the God-given right to control how she lives and behaves. Her needs or thoughts were not even considered. There was never a sense of mutuality or loving consideration. It was always his way, or nothing. Rosemarie would have found that she no longer associated with certain friends, groups, or even family members because of her need to keep him happy. Even though these activities or people were important to her, she found herself preferring to avoid them in order to keep the peace.

'From the outset of their relationship he believed – and acted – as if her opinions, views, feelings, or thoughts had no real value. He discredited them on principle or, specifically, because she was a woman and easily deceived. His psychopathy allows him to wear a mask of respectability and charm on some occasions – at work, at the guest house, in front of officials – yet at home the whole family had to walk on eggshells to prevent setting him off. People who did not see him at home may have found it hard to believe that Rosemarie really was suffering emotional abuse.

'She felt confused by his behaviour because one day he could be loving, kind, charming, and gentle; the next day cruel and full of rage. The switch seemed to come without warning, no matter how much she tried to improve or change in her relationship with him: she always felt confused, inadequate, guilty, and somehow off balance. She never knew what would set him off next and, no matter how much she prayed, he never changed. Fritzl's ego was so monstrous that he would actually have portrayed himself as virtuous for putting up with her. A unique feature of misogyny like his is that its abusive, non-empathetic grandiosity is directed towards the women in their lives – first Rosemarie, later Elisabeth. Extremely control oriented, he needed to control and dominate his wife, and later his daughter.

'From comments his own relatives have made, he made sex mechanical (when and where he wanted it), refused to be concerned about her sexual satisfaction, became less and less physically affectionate within a short period of time after marriage and expressed repulsion or disgust at the idea of romantically touching her in public – indeed, in private for much of the time. The goal of his emotional and psychological battering was to wear down his wife, to keep her under his control at all costs. Yelling, bullying, threatening, temper tantrums, name calling, constant criticism, verbal attacks, ridiculing the woman's pain, subtle attempts to confuse her and make her doubt her sanity, forgetting things that happened between them, accusations, blaming, and rewriting history – these were the tactics he used.'

Rosemarie felt an emotional attachment to her husband that allowed her to survive more than half a century of marital abuse. It would be many years later that she would receive the care she needed and see the doctors who would tell her she was not worthless, that she had merit, that she did not deserve the abuse – physical or verbal –

meted out to her by her husband. But by then, it would be too late. Of all Josef Fritzl's victims, her sufferings were the most prolonged, keeping her in thrall to a man whose monstrous tyranny overshadowed her life.

3. How Do You Solve a Problem Like Elisabeth?

The place smelled of urine and the stone floor was cold. The girls wrapped themselves up as best they could in their sleeping bags, one promising to stay awake while the other slept and vice versa. A chill wind whipped up empty crisp packets and torn newspaper sheets, sending them flurrying upwards in little tornadoes. The runaways had been on the loose for a week and their dreams of finding work and refuge had disintegrated into living like tramps. They were dirty, tired, hungry and dispirited; there were no pots of gold in Vienna, just a hard-edged city with unfriendly faces and predatory men. Mascara was smudged on their tired faces. They had made a pledge to find a public lavatory the next morning to have a decent wash. Still, the railway station was better than where they had kipped down three nights previously; that had been inside a foul-smelling toilet at the edge of a park.

One of the girls was angry, her face a mask of irritation. It had seemed like an adventure just days ago to pack up and run away. The excitement had dwindled with their meagre savings. 'I don't know why I listened to you in the first place,' she said. 'I think we should pack it in, go home, say sorry and get a life again.'

'Easy for you to say,' said the other girl, Elisabeth Fritzl. 'You know why I can't go home . . .'

*

When did it start? When did the feelings cross the line, from the unseemly thought to the horrific act? What propelled Josef Fritzl to come to regard his own daughter as a sexual object who was there solely to pleasure him and provide for him the secret fantasy family he dreamed of? How did Liesl, as all the family members call her, come to deserve such a fate?

Arrogance, allied to lust and magnified by obsession, lured Josef Fritzl's diseased mind into the darkest of places. His companion on the journey was doomed to be his favourite daughter, who edged out his mother to become the target of all his warped fantasies. Incest, a universal taboo, has evolved over millennia and means different things in different societies. For westerners, it is generally understood as breaching the laws prohibiting sex or marriage with a closely related person (in Fritzl's case, father–daughter). It is, above all, an abuse of power, whereby the stronger person objectifies the other, devaluing them without empathy for their feelings. When Josef Fritzl decided to begin raping his daughter, it was for his gratification alone. There was no thought in his head of the terrible consequences his actions would have for Liesl.

It was a long road leading to 28 August, 1984, the day when Fritzl would put his master plan into action. It involved planning, it involved scheming, it involved duplicity and deception of a high order, and the cool nerves to pull it off. It involved secrets, lies, arrogance and utter self-belief. And it required the crossing of the Rubicon of moral and societal boundaries. This was the triumph of Josef Fritzl's will; that he could make a case for what he was doing and live with it, more or less happily, for the next 24 years.

The fate of Elisabeth appears to lie both in her beauty and her wilfulness. It is the notion of fathers everywhere to lock up their daughters when they start transforming from shapeless young girls into shapely young women, to protect themselves as much as their children's virtue when the bad boys start calling for a date. It was Elisabeth's misfortune to have a father who had no problem whatsoever in turning a notion into a depraved reality.

Elisabeth was a child who offended the 'order, discipline, obedience' mantra that came to define Fritzl's life. Even when she was only 12, when police said her father began constructing the cellar in which he would keep her, his Nazi-era mindset married to his unstoppable mania for control led him to despise his fun-loving daughter's ways. Given that so much planning went into building the cellar lair, Fritzl's later admission that he had shut her away from the outside world to protect her from herself, from running around with the 'loose set', smoking, drinking and partying, should be treated with derision. She was earmarked to be a captive sex slave long before the first filter tip ever reached her lips. 'My father chose me for himself,' she would later tell police, and that at an unseemly young age.

Elfriede Hoera, who helped Rosemarie so often at the Mondsee site, witnessed at first hand his need to exert total control over his daughter. She spoke about her fears for Elisabeth in exclusive interviews for this book. 'Our children often used to play together down at Mondsee. The older children were allowed to play together more than the younger ones whom he controlled more. Usually parents are stricter with older children and become more relaxed as they have more children and acquire more confidence in dealing with their kids. I thought it was strange that he was so obsessive over controlling what the younger children did, especially Elisabeth. I noticed that Elisabeth tended to be given the role of looking after the younger children. She was very good with young children, seemed to genuinely care about them.

'Her father? Well, he was called a tyrant at home and that's a pretty accurate description. He ruled everybody with an iron fist. That included his wife. But she was completely trapped, in that she had seven children with him and they were everything to her. She couldn't leave them – it wasn't possible for her to even consider it. So she just got on with it. I'm positive she knew nothing about what was going on with Elisabeth. She was so busy, she wouldn't have had a lot of time for reflection on her own life.

'Her eldest daughter, Ulli, was a very serious child; she studied hard and did everything her mother and father wanted. She is a teacher now. The second daughter, Rosemarie, was much more of a free spirit. Elisabeth you can only characterize as being painfully shy. All the others were far more open in various ways. In retrospect, I am sure he was abusing her before she went into the cellar. He says it started in the cellar, but it was definitely before that. Why else was she so shy?

'She was very pretty, blondish, and she took a lot more beatings than the rest. I know my sons had a bit of a crush on her, but she was always very correct. She certainly didn't let any of them get too close. She didn't seem to want any particularly close friendships. The one passion was the children – her younger siblings. It was the one time I ever saw her really open up. Of all the girls Ulli was never hit, Rosemarie a bit, although she was the naughtiest, and Elisabeth constantly.

'She seemed to try and blend into the background all the time, especially when he was around, but he always singled her out for a hiding. I once commented on it to Rosemarie and she told me: "He just doesn't seem to like her. I don't know why but he just doesn't." Rosemarie indicated to me, in conversations but also in things left unsaid, that she would have liked to have gone away. She thought if she left she wouldn't be able to take the children with her and so she stayed in order to better protect them. She took beatings from him too, I know.

'I once asked her why she put up with it. She said: "What can I do? I have to be strong for the children." She was really just a working animal for him. He didn't care about her. She always had to work. And lots. With regards to their sex life, I don't know what went on. I mean, they had seven children, and they'd been married a long time, so it wouldn't surprise me if there wasn't a lot happening in that area by the time we knew them.'

Elfriede's daughter Helga, now 48, was a friend of Elisabeth's. She remembers: 'We met at Mondsee. I was a bit older than Liesl but we used to both get nursery duty; we both liked looking after the kids. At the end of one summer I was given 100 German marks from Fritzl, for helping out with holidaymakers' kids and stuff – I remember it because, while I was really happy, my dad was annoyed. He accused Josef of ripping me off.

'I was allowed to go once to Ybbsstrasse for a week; there was scaffolding everywhere, and I had to look after the younger ones with Elisabeth. I was 14 and she was at school by then. I remember the kids didn't have much in the way of toys, and they had to share a bed. I had to squeeze in with them all.'

She recalls Fritzl as being friendly enough, to her, but strict to his own kids. 'I saw the mask slip once when he lost his temper over something, I forget what, and he wanted to hit them. But Rosemarie threw herself between them – they would hide behind her, peering out. I was more cautious of him after that.'

It was a scene all too common for Fritzl's own children, and especially Elisabeth. The beatings started early on in life, as punishment for any transgressions against his rigid code. Elisabeth's room was untidy; out came the belt. The stairs not swept, the command not answered, the dress not clean, the homework not done. Fritzl resorted to the fist and the slap of leather every time. The carefree lass was reduced to a whipped cur, tiptoeing around a house that was a fortress of fear, both for her and her friends. They recall always having to leave when Fritzl came home – the turn of the key in the door was a noise which drained the blood from the face of a little girl whose eyes were daily draining of hope, even as her life stretched before her.

Still living in Amstetten, not far from Ybbsstrasse 40, is former classmate Susanne Parb, like Elisabeth now aged 42. She says: 'I was at school with Elisabeth for 5 years, the 4 years of secondary school and then one year at the polytechnic, both in Amstetten. I remember that she was always very afraid of her father; she was always worried that she would come home just a couple of minutes too late. Usually, she left to go home just after the bell rang; she never stayed around after school with the other students. Once I went to the library with her; she looked at her watch and realized that she was already supposed to be home, so she immediately left. She was always looking at her watch at the end of the day, checking the time, making sure the watch was working.

'You could see that her father was a tyrant at home, and that she wasn't allowed to do anything. I sometimes asked Elisabeth why she let her father do that to her, because I wasn't used to this kind of upbringing. She said that she wasn't allowed to question any of the decisions and orders made by her parents. I'd been to her place a few times, but I could feel that I wasn't very welcome there.

'While we went to secondary school, Elisabeth never seemed to be interested in boys at all. That was a bit unusual, but not too noticeable as there were always people who were rather quiet and shy, and she was definitely one of them. In our last year together, at the polytechnic, I had the impression that she would've liked to have a boyfriend, but she was worried about it maybe going beyond a bit of kissing. She was a pretty girl, though – she had long, thick hair and was quite light skinned. One day, I went to her place with two boys when nobody was at home. When I think about it now, I'm still glad that her father didn't come home then. We'd been sitting together with the boys at the bus stop outside school and we were just joking around. After a while we thought that it would be nice to go somewhere else, so Elisabeth suggested we go to her place to get something to drink as she lived just around the corner.

'She must have known that her parents weren't at home, otherwise she'd have never been able to bring boys back to her place and take them to her room. Back then, friends had told me a story about being at Elisabeth's place. For her twelfth or thirteenth birthday she had some friends over for a little birthday party. Her mother, Rosemarie, was there, taking care of them, but then she suddenly came into the room and said, "Quick, everybody must go home right now, your father is coming home."

'At school Elisabeth never talked about her family; the only brother she ever mentioned was Harald. He was just a year older than us, so I got to know him as well. I think that he was very afraid of his father too. He once said when he didn't pay attention to his father, and he'd been given a bad mark, that he knew what would happen and was going to hide. He said: "I'm not stupid, I'm not going home right now to get a beating." As far as I know, Harald did the same as all the older children and left home to get married as soon as it was possible.'

In fact only Josef Fritzl junior failed to leave the nest, increasingly taking over the jobs and tasks his father allotted to him as more and more of his siblings left. Eventually he became a full-time janitor, cleaner and assistant at their guest houses, and a labourer on their building sites. But always in a subordinate role, never in charge. There could only ever be one man in control, and that was Josef Fritzl senior.

Susanne believes Elisabeth was about to leave and would have had a good life, like the rest of her siblings: 'I think that Elisabeth would have left as well, and that was the reason for him to lock her up. She had already run away to Vienna once while she was training to be a waitress at a motorway service station at Strengberg. That's where she worked after we finished school, at 15. We had pretty much lost contact then as I went to Vienna to work and, when I came back home to Amstetten, I used to go out a lot. A couple of years later, I met Harald again and I asked how Elisabeth was doing. He said she'd run away to join an unknown sect, and that she'd even been searched for by Interpol. I was shocked, but it sounded logical to me as I could understand why she would've wanted to get away from home. Unfortunately, domestic violence and sexual abuse within families was something never talked about back then. Elisabeth would've never said a word, and you could never see any signs like her having bruises somewhere on her body. Especially after she'd run away for the first time, the family should've been checked by a psychologist.

'Three years ago, there was a class reunion with the people from school. The lady who organized the event told us that Elisabeth had run away so many years ago and had left three children at her parents' doorstep. She hadn't been aware of that, and so she'd tried to invite Elisabeth to the reunion as well. As she couldn't track down an address for her, she went to her parents' place, where she met Rosemarie and asked her about her daughter. Rosemarie then told her the story and said that she didn't know anything about her at all. She was crying as she told the story – I mean, really distressed.

'I have some relatives who know someone who works at the clinic in Mauer where Elisabeth and her children are staying now, and I heard that Elisabeth is a very strong woman, who has her children under control – they love her and respect her.

'I went to her house a few times to play when we were very young, but not when the father was there. He didn't like me because I asked questions about why Elisabeth couldn't leave and come to mine for dinner. Soon he banned me from meeting her. Elisabeth didn't seem sad at school but was just very quiet. She had a good relationship with her brother Harald and her younger sister Doris.'

At her daughter's side, Susanne Parb's mother, Brigitte, adds: 'When it all came out I realized I couldn't remember Elisabeth ever visiting my daughter at all. I guess she wasn't allowed to, as there were many other friends of hers coming over all the time. Most people in Amstetten of course knew about the story, about Fritzl being a convicted sex offender. But we never heard anything concrete, most of the things the people were saying were just rumours. All in all, we always thought that it might be true that Elisabeth had run away as her father was the sort of person you ran away from. But that he had locked her up – never did it enter my wildest imaginings.'

Not far away from Ybbsstrasse is the bus stop where Elisabeth used to shelter from view with pals in the final minutes before she had to either go home or set off for school. There are no children there when Christa

Woldrich, then known as one of the Götzinger twins and another of Elisabeth's school friends, takes a seat. It is in the centre of Amstetten, a nowhere town whose name is destined to join the almanac of infamous places world-wide where terrible things have happened. It is just six weeks on from the liberation of the Fritzl victims. Christa knows the world sees Elisabeth as a victim, a refugee from a world of darkness and pain. Yet closing her eyes and taking a breath, she recalls how easy it is to imagine her former best friend sitting next to her, fresh-faced and alert, at the same spot where they waited to go to school together, in the life Elisabeth once had. At this same bus stop the pair waited every morning, chatting about boys, make-up, teachers, television.

She sits down and puts her hands on the sides of the seats, grabbing them firmly as she recalls the time she spent with her friend. It is the first time she has spoken about her in years and it is painful to revisit Elisabeth's youth. 'We bonded well at school. We had things in common – strict families, not too much spare cash in the home. That meant we both started off the week with fresh clothes on a Monday and we were still wearing them on Friday. That provoked its own brand of insults from the other kids, you can imagine. We both thought of ourselves as outsiders. I suppose we found it a little difficult to mix with other children. That made us, in turn, very close and some of the other kids didn't like it, called us names like "lesbian", although that was rubbish. Being outcasts suited us fine. In five years we shared everything, or so I thought, but I never realized the truth about what was happening to her at home.'

'Their time together outside school was limited, Christa says, due mostly to Elisabeth's need to get home as soon as possible so as not to upset her father. 'But we'd talk together at every chance we had and grew very close. We'd walk home together after school, sometimes stopping at a nearby shop to buy sweets when we had the money. Elisabeth's favourite was sherbet powder, I remember. Elisabeth always had to be home at the latest half an hour after school had finished. Then she had to do her homework and study, just like me.

'I don't think I would ever have guessed what was happening to her. She wasn't a particularly sad child. But I was never allowed to visit her. The only explanation she ever gave was that her father was very strict. I didn't see him, but he was always there between us because of his influence over her, like an invisible presence that you could always feel, even if you didn't clap eyes on him.

'Elisabeth never had a boyfriend and she was never close to having one when we knew each other, up until we were 16 or so. It's hard to say, but I think she would've never got near a "normal sex life", bearing in mind she was probably raped from the age of 11. We never talked about sex. This just never came into our minds; it wasn't a topic.

'Elisabeth was an average student, as far as her marks and efforts were concerned. Furthermore, she was never involved in playing jokes on the teachers – and we did that a lot. I don't know whether she wanted to be a mother. We never talked about it, but I assume she wanted to be one, some day. When I finished school my plan was to take up an apprenticeship in Tyrol. I rarely saw her at that time but planned to say goodbye to her. In the end, I didn't meet her to do that. Now I know I'll regret this for the rest of my life.

'I know it's hard to imagine any child being abused but, if you knew Elisabeth, it's even harder to fathom. She had an innate kindness in her, a gentleness towards all things. She loved animals and nature, butterflies, spiders. She would tell the nasty boy at school off if she saw him hurt a fly. To think someone had taken something so pure and then corrupted it sickens me to the pit of my stomach. And to think she had no one to turn to. She endured all the terror of growing up, perhaps keeping herself going with the knowledge that soon she would be able to leave home and get a life, and then the axe fell and he beheaded her. What a total bastard.

'Her favourite singer from back then was Shakin' Stevens, but we liked all the English singers. We used to try and understand the lyrics. We were together for four years at the secondary school on Pestalozzistrasse. We were also together for a year at the polytechnic. My parents had a tobacconist's so I would get us cigarettes. At the weekend I know she used to watch a lot of TV – *The Boy Who Sold His Smile* was a series she liked. She was never allowed out with us. I only ever saw her at church at the weekend. Other than that she was always kept at home. Neither of us ever had any money – for her it was because her dad didn't want her to have any, for me it was because my parents didn't have any.

'We were both pretty average at school. I don't think she took any pleasure in school work, was always a bit distant – she didn't like German or maths, but we both enjoyed sports. Volleyball and swimming were our favourites. To think that someone who liked physical exertion would have to be practically immobile for so many years just beggars belief.'

Jutta Haberci, Christa's twin sister, spent five years in the same class as Elisabeth at secondary school and polytechnic. She is ill at ease in her Poysdorf flat as she looks back on their friendship. 'I don't think anyone would have guessed that she was being abused. I never really noticed anything, but of course I knew, we all knew, that she was never allowed visitors at home. In all of the years I knew her she was never allowed to come to us for a weekend or anything. She never went on school trips; she was like some prisoner who was allowed out only at specific times and only with the express permission of her father. She lived in fear of him, we knew that much. She was a good-looking girl and, if all this was going on at home, she certainly hid it. We were both good friends with her, me and my sister.

'She did pretty well in lessons, not a genius, but OK. She never had the latest clothing or anything like that – there were a few people at school, I suppose, who clearly had more money. I only saw her infamous dad once. I was near her house and decided I wanted to visit her. I knocked on the door and her mother opened it, and I went into the hallway. She was quite normal; she told me to wait a minute. Suddenly he was there, towering over me, his eyes looking at me as if I'd stepped in something nasty and scraped it on his carpet. He was really rude; he just looked at me and said, "You – get out." He never asked what I wanted. It wasn't like I had history with him

– he was just a tyrant. That was what Sissy, as her friends always called her, said he was like and that was what he was. I told her about it the next day. I said I'd been there, I'd met her dad and he'd thrown me out. She just said . . . nothing. Just listened, didn't react in any way at all. In hindsight, I think she was too scared to say anything that might encourage me to come back again. I imagine he probably gave her a hard time about her friends coming to visit.

'One sensed that something was wrong – as children you do – but I couldn't have said it was child abuse. I guess that's the way of abusers – it's hidden and they terrify the child into keeping the secret. I know he was hard on all the kids when it came to discipline. My brother Karl was very pally with Harald. Harald said his father used to beat him and that "life was hard" in that home.

'I saw after Elisabeth resurfaced that her dad said he wanted to stop her "wild ways". Well, I don't know about wild. I know she and my sis used to puff ciggies at the bus stop while they were waiting to go to school. I used to keep a watch out in case teachers or parents came by. She wasn't allowed to wear make-up at home but, like a lot of the girls, used to put a bit on when she got to school; not a tarty look, just a little bit here and there, made her feel better, a bit more feminine, I suppose. After the final bell she went into the toilets to scrub it all off, to make sure her old man didn't see it.

'During our last year at school we used to hang around a club called the Turk's Cellar in Amstetten. We got a lot of free lessons so, as it was technically school time and she didn't have to rush back home to keep him happy, she would come along. There was a lot of flirting with boys but she never had a boyfriend as such – at least, not one I ever knew about. Elisabeth was closer to my sister in that respect because she didn't have a fella either, and so they knocked around together a lot. I hope that Elisabeth remembered some of those happy times in the Turk's Cellar, because she was on her own for an awfully long time with an awfully scary monster. Perhaps, just perhaps, she remembered dancing to Duran Duran and puffing on a ciggie and flashing her eyes at the lads, and it might have given her some courage. Poor Sissy. She was a lovely girl . . .'

Alfred Dubanovsky was also at school with Elisabeth, and a tenant with his family at Ybbsstrasse 40. Like everyone who knew her then he scours his memory banks for warning signs he thinks he may have missed, for any telltale signs of abuse he failed to spot back then. 'We were in the same class and we were friends. We used to spend a lot of time together. She was a great girl, but very shy and pretty nervous; you needed to know her before she would trust you. But we got on really well, we'd even danced together a couple of times. I had a bit of a crush on her but it never went any further. I mean, she was rarely allowed any free time to get to know any boys. We all used to go to the Belami disco on her road, Ybbsstrasse, but she was rarely allowed out to see us.

'After she vanished we were talking about it, and we knew she'd run off before. We thought she'd run off again because she'd told someone in our group that she'd had enough, couldn't stand it any more at home, and that her father had beaten her, and had hurt her. She said she was scared of him.'

Another friend of Elisabeth's, who refuses to be identified, claims that Fritzl punched his children. 'He didn't slap or spank them,' says the friend. 'He hit them with his fists. Her brother once told me, "The pig will beat us to death one day."'

Elisabeth's hopes of escape, and her first experiences of life away from home, came when she landed an apprenticeship as a waitress that began at a motorway service station at Strengberg after finishing school at 15. It was a three-year apprenticeship that included on-the-job training, time away from home at a tourism school in Waldegg near Wiener Neustadt, south of Vienna – and 240 kilometres away from her father – and also some time as a waitress in Tyrol. She had switched her place of work to Tyrol because it was further from Amstetten and her abusive father, but she was still obliged to return home and remain under his control because she was not yet 18.

Susanne Parb adds: 'Elisabeth used to say, "It would be great if only I could escape. I can't wait for the day when I'll be free of him." As soon as she got the job in the motorway service station restaurant she started saving money. Her plan was to leave when she was 18 because then he couldn't force her to come back home. She had her bag packed and was bracing herself to say goodbye to her mother when she vanished. It made sense that she had run off to join a cult because everyone knew she lived in fear of her father. Before she vanished Elisabeth told me she was beaten very badly at home. Her father was clever, though, and made sure he didn't hit her where anyone could see the bruises – that's why the teachers didn't know. But Elisabeth never spoke about the rapes. I think she must have been very ashamed.'

Unfortunately the ties that bind were the ties that blind; no one knew the ultimate horror of what was occurring except Elisabeth and her father. She was even left alone on occasions to stay with him as her sisters were taken away by Rosemarie to enjoy a summer holiday. Photos in this book show two sisters enjoying an idyllic break – lying in the sun, taking boat trips, swimming in azure-blue pools. Teenagers Ulrike and Rosemarie Fritzl were miles away as 11-year-old Liesl was with her father, enduring who knows what. It was part of his manipulative character to create situations where he could be alone with her, to allow the abuse to continue without risk of accidental discovery.

Frau Danielczyk, the neighbour from across the street, says Rosemarie was no help to Elisabeth, petrified as she was whenever the father of her children was around. 'Rosemarie would often come round and sit here, talking to me, when he wasn't there,' she remembers. 'She would sit by the window and watch to see when he came home. She was relaxed and happy and chatty when he wasn't there – but as soon as he came back, she left you straight away and rushed over the road to him.

'The one incident that sticks in my mind was when I was talking to her over the garden hedge. I don't think he saw that I was there and he came into the garden bellowing and shouting and in a temper. He was demanding to know where his lunch was and asking if he would have to wait until 1.30 p.m. before he got to eat it. There were oaths and swearing and dark threats about "sorting you out later". Later on I spoke to him when his wife was there and I apologized for detaining her when she had other things to do. The mask was back in place; he laughed and made a joke of it and said there had been no problem. You would never have guessed that the person raging about his food and the man standing in front of me were one and the same.

'Elisabeth suffered at his hands. He would shout at her: "You will obey me or, so help me God, I will break your back." Later, when she vanished, he would shrug and say, well, she was 18, of course, and he had done his "absolute best" for her. I know a lot of people have said Rosemarie must have known what was going on, but I am absolutely convinced she had no idea. Her life was very full cooking and cleaning and catering for her own children's needs. And also of course, she was always worried about making sure Fritzl was happy. I don't think she ever had the time really to stop and dwell on Elisabeth.

'You know, she really was a caring child. One day she found kittens in her garden and fed them by hand. But he made her give them away. She often played ball in the garden too, with her brothers and sisters. That all stopped around about the age of 11. Then she became even more shy and introverted. I think we know why now . . .'

Paul Hoera, the pal from Mondsee who has known the family for 35 years, recalls: 'My three children always played with his children, although I remember that Elisabeth as a child was very withdrawn and shy. I got the impression that he didn't like her very much; he didn't treat her as well as the other children. He used to beat her a lot more than them as well. She used to get a slap for every small thing.'

His daughter Helga adds: 'Ulli was his favourite.' She says Fritzl's eldest child fitted in with his ideals for order, obedience and respect. 'Rosie was a rebel, she was always sneaking out to meet boys and go to the local disco, she was a free spirit and loads of fun.'

Her dad agrees, saying: 'I had a pet dog at Mondsee, a dachshund, and it ate some rat poison that Josef had put down. I'd gone to see him and he said, "Bloody hell, your dog's just eaten the rat poison." I didn't know what to do and Rosie was there and said she'd come with me to the vet's and show me where it was. Her dad told her she was staying there and she had work to do, but she just told him to get lost and she was going anyway. She said, "Come on, Paul, let's go." She was great like that. I know he didn't want her to go away on holiday, but she just put her foot down and that was that – she was allowed to go.'

A friend of the Fritzl sisters went on the holiday with them and provided the snaps. She says: 'I can't bear to see them any more – while we were enjoying ourselves, he could have been at home putting Elisabeth through who knows what ordeal.'

Elisabeth's former teacher Karl Ostertag was part of the adult world that ultimately failed Elisabeth. Neither he nor others spotted the silent despair in which she lived. No one noticed the warning signs which signalled a girl in danger. 'I taught Elisabeth for three years at the tourism and catering school at Waldegg near Wiener Neustadt as she planned a career in catering. She was a great pupil, smart and with a bright future ahead of her. She had completed three years of her studies, including a final exam for a career in the catering industry.

'What I remember about her is that at the weekend she always opted to stay here rather than go home. We did have some places for boarding students – and she had one of them. If she was sexually abused from the age of 11 onwards, then of course I now understand her reluctance to go home. But I never had an inkling.

'I guess I remember her better than other students from this time because I was often on duty at the weekends to keep an eye on the students. I used to take two or three of my own children with me. One of our sons, he was five, six years old at the time, he totally adored her. She was really great with children and I remember there was no one else my son liked as much.

'One incident sticks in my mind; for his sixth birthday the only thing he wanted more than anything else was to go for lunch to the restaurant she was working in. We had a party there. She was such a nice girl. I often ask myself over the years how I could have been so wrong about her. I now know that I did her a great injustice.'

It is clear that Fritzl was able to begin the abuse, and continue with it, because his daughter matched the pattern of victims the world over. All child abuse experts say children find it difficult to tell anyone they have been abused. They often feel shame and are told by their abusers they will be hated, rejected, or disbelieved if they tell. Also, if the abuser threatens the child or someone the child loves, the child may not question the abuser's power to carry out the threat. Elisabeth wanted to tell of the abuse so it could stop, but feared she would not be believed or protected. Many child victims like her have been known to keep details of incest bottled up for years, not disclosing the full extent of their pain and fear until adulthood, if at all. Fritzl manipulated his victim by enforcing secrecy; he created a sense of fear, destroying any privacy and security provided by family.

Less than two per cent of all investigated incest allegations worldwide prove to be false, according to research conducted in America. Given that Elisabeth Fritzl had an Everest of crimes to pin on her father after she regained her freedom, it seems inconceivable that she might lie about this early stage of her life. Police officers and those who have spoken for the purposes of this book say they have no reason to disbelieve what she said her father did to her, and when he did it.

Elisabeth suffered in silence as a schoolgirl, just as she would later suffer in silence in the cellar as her father's captive. Sigrun Rossmanith, an Austrian court psychiatrist, concludes that Fritzl developed dual personalities. One was the hard-but-fair family man who encouraged politeness, deference and manners in others – specifically, his wife and children – and the other was a tyrant with a compulsive need for total control, particularly over women. The zenith of his power complex manifested itself in Elisabeth. Frau Rossmanith explains: 'She was a slave that he could use at any moment of his choosing. He made her submissive and used her according to his needs. He exercised absolute control over her.'

Family, friends and relations say her siblings intuited their father's moods and wants far better than Elisabeth.

She may have been shy, but she was strong, proud and possessed an independent spirit; a dangerous trinity for the man who only ever wanted his children to obey him. Her treatment caused consternation for her mother, who worried about her daughter. But Rosemarie, as Frau Hoera witnessed, was impotent in the shadow of her husband. She was as cowed as everyone else, able to do little more than take the knocks he would otherwise have aimed at her children.

Years later, with Elisabeth finally free of his gravitational pull, her aunt Christine paints a disturbing portrait of life within Fortress Fritzl. 'She – Rosi – never believed him capable of it. After she vanished, I mean. We spoke about it often when we met. And I would say, "Rosemarie, where can Elisabeth be?"'

'She was married to a tyrant who created a culture of fear in his home. When he said it was black, it was black, even when it was ten times white. He tolerated no dissent. Listen, if I myself was scared of him at a family party, and I didn't feel confident to say anything in any form that could possibly offend him, then you can imagine how it must have been for a woman who spent so many years with him.

'We were all taken in by him. Every person who looked in his eyes was fooled by him.'

Even when he was caged for rape in 1967, Rosemarie chose to look away; she chose to think the best of 'Sepp' and told anyone who asked that the authorities had 'made a mistake'.

Privately, thinks Christine, the relationship changed and soured after his conviction, yet convention and

Catholicism, family pride and circumstance, led them to carry on with the façade of respectability and contentment. 'As far as I know no sex took place in recent years between them. I believe it was because of his prior conviction, and because my sister had been getting bigger. And in any case, he never liked fat women.'

Still, she could not see any warning signs that something was wrong in the relationship between Elisabeth and her father. 'He was just as strict with her as he was with every other child. There was nothing in particular that could lead you to say he was more intimate with her. From the child as well, it never came out. She never confided in anyone.'

When, at 15, Elisabeth finally landed her place on the course to become a trainee waitress, she must have hoped it was her ticket to freedom, her liberation from abuse. She wrote to a friend of how 'grown up' she felt; with her money from the programme, she hoped to be able to take a long holiday in Italy or France.

'She was so quiet and nice to everyone,' says Franz Hochwallner, a cook who worked with Elisabeth. 'She was beautiful, a charming girl. Yet there was an underlying sadness. When we finished the day's work and chatted about life and families and hopes, she seemed to clam up. It was territory that she clearly didn't like visiting.'

But Elisabeth was not yet old enough to be able to leave home and live independently; under Austrian law, she was bound to her parents until her eighteenth birthday. She had to return home – and there is no reason to suppose the abuse stopped.

*

On January 28, 1983, Elisabeth ran away from home and, together with another girl from work, went to Vienna, where she lived in hiding in the city's 20th District. The name of the other girl who fled with her has not been revealed; she is determined to remain anonymous because she hopes to be reunited with Elisabeth and to avoid being seen as part of the media circus that continues to swirl around the Fritzl clan.

Yet part of her story has been told to this book by a friend of hers who knew Fritzl up close, a former tenant of his called Josef 'Sepp' Leitner, a 43-year-old night-club manager who rented one of the Fritzl flats. He says: 'Now that the full story has come out my friend is absolutely distraught; she is having to have psychological counselling herself. She can't really deal with it. She thought Elisabeth might be dead or a drug addict or a prostitute. She imagined all sorts of terrible things, but nothing as terrible as what really happened. My friend thinks Fritzl knew Elisabeth would beat it out of there as soon as she turned 18, and that he wouldn't be able to get her back.

'She doesn't want to talk to the media, and she really does want to meet Elisabeth eventually. They haven't allowed it yet, but she's still hoping that it might happen. The media have offered me a lot of money for her to speak, but she won't do it. She'd see it as the final betrayal of a woman who has been betrayed too much already in her life. It was from her that I heard Elisabeth had been raped by her father. When I moved into the flat back in the 90s, I told this girl where I was living. She was horrified when she recognized the address and said: "You can't be serious! Are you mad? Do you know who this arsehole is? He raped his own daughter – Sissy."

'My friend told me about the first time she and Elisabeth ran away. Sissy begged her to go with her. She said she had had enough, enough of him fiddling with her, beating her, seeing her mum cowed by him. All human beings, I guess, have a breaking point and Elisabeth was close to it. My friend wasn't particularly happy or unhappy at home but she decided to join her, thought that it was the least she could do as Sissy was so low. They had all sorts of vague notions of hitting the big time in Vienna, getting work, getting an apartment. Of course none of it was thought through, and they ended up like a couple of dossers.

'Fritzl went completely mad, kicked up a huge fuss, demanded the police call Interpol. He went to the local paper and they ran a story about her. He said she had fallen in with a "bad crowd", mentioned drugs and drink – although the Sissy I knew had never taken drugs – and that he only wanted her safely back in the family. He was obsessed about having her back under his control again. He got in his car and drove everywhere he could think of and spoke to everybody, trying to find her. He was obsessed. After three weeks he finally got her back again. The girls made a mistake; they didn't have any way of supporting themselves and had been relying on the goodwill of people they met. They were living in the city's 20th District, a sprawling, anonymous area of tower blocks intersected by railway yards and warehouses – not the best of areas, but not the worst either. Just grey and anonymous.

'Because they had no serious cash, they couldn't put down the deposit to rent a flat. They moved in a sort of anarchist-student circle, crashing out where they could, relying on the charity of others. But they also had to sleep rough; my friend told me of a night in the subway that really spooked her. She was all for returning home; in the end, though, she didn't have to make the decision.

'They got invited back to a party, which they readily accepted as it might mean the chance of sleeping on a sofa, or perhaps even a bed. Anyway, this night, they'd drunk too much and the music had been too loud, and a neighbour had called the police, who demanded to be let in and asked to see everyone's ID. The cops saw how young the two girls were and took them back to the station, where they checked their identities and then called Fritzl. The Viennese police banged them both up for the night, let them sleep off the booze, and the next day Fritzl drove to the city to collect them.

'He really terrorized my friend on the return journey, said she was never to see Elisabeth again. But then they bumped into each other again in town – I mean, it's not a big place here in Amstetten – and the contact started again. Sissy begged my friend to go away with her, but by then she'd started a new life with a new group of friends and a new job and didn't want to have to go through such an awful ordeal again. My friend was cured of the vagabond life after that, but not Sissy; she would've done anything rather than return home to her awful father. My friend told Elisabeth: "I've got a boyfriend now and a new life." It was a hard time for two girls aged just 16.

'Someone in authority should have asked why the girls

ran away, instead of just handing them back to their parents. I mean, she was a kid on the edge. I know, for example, that she swallowed some sleeping pills the week before she went away – whether it was a cry for help or a real attempt to end it all, I just don't know. Clearly, she was ready to blow. But there was no psychiatrist or psychologist who was asked to look into their backgrounds. They just handed them back. Elisabeth ran away because she wanted to get away from her abusive father, and my friend went with her because they were best friends and she wanted to help her.'

According to family insiders, this was not the first time Elisabeth had bolted; there had been a half-hearted attempt to get away when she was 15, involving a hitched ride to Linz and a couple of nights on her own wandering around. But this time, this brazen attempt to get away from him, triggered in her father a new determination that she would never again slip away from his grasp. When she returned home in the third week of February 1983 she would have barely 18 more months of freedom before disappearing into his man-made underworld.

In getting away from his orbit Elisabeth had unwittingly written a large part of the script that Fritzl would later use to explain her prolonged disappearance. 'Well,' he told Paul Hoera, 'she's a bad 'un, isn't she, Paul? I mean, look at what happened last year – off to Vienna, smoking, drinking, whoring for all I know. It's her poor mother I worry about, drives her to distraction. All we ever tried to do was our best for her, but you can't help some people, can you? You just can't help some people . . .'

PART TWO
Martyrdom

4. The Vanishing

The final touches were put to it: the grouting smoothed on the tiles, the floor laid, the cooker installed, the toilet plumbed. The electricity was being paid for by other tenants, via Fritzl's canny knack of wiring the place up to be powered by the individual flats above. The shower was functioning, and the deep freeze too. Waste water was plumbed into the main house system, as was the toilet; the majority of rubbish would be taken care of by the powerful solid-fuel burner that heated the place. Whatever could not be burned would be hauled up to the surface under cover of night.

Fritzl allowed himself a chuckle; advertise this in the local paper, knock off a few euros for the lack of a view, and he reckoned he could rent it out to Americans on European jaunts. Yet it was destined to only have one occupant. Full board, views limited, very quiet. Length of stay: indefinite.

It had cost the equivalent of £80,000 pounds – some of it in the form of a grant from the local council – and hundreds of man-hours to construct this room, as well as those which led to it and masked its existence. Fritzl had first dreamed of creating the cellar in 1978, six years before he moved in the young woman he had defiled since childhood. He was proud of what he'd made – what engineer wouldn't be? It was his kingdom and, as supreme

ruler, he felt happy. He went upstairs when his children
and Rosemarie were not around and grabbed the hi-fi
that belonged to his son Harald, the son who was closest
to the daughter he coveted. He sneaked it back into
the cellar, together with a heavy-metal record from his
collection, switched it on and played it at full blast. Then
he retreated back through the maze of doors to the outside
world, where he pretended to scrutinize his garden, his ears
straining all the while to see if he could hear a sound. As
police officers found when they performed the same
experiment with microphones and loudspeakers 24 years
later, there was not a sound to be heard. Perfect.

The cellar which the world saw, the windowless warren
with sleeping chambers carved beneath the grounds of
the Fritzl home, was not the one in which Elisabeth
was initially imprisoned. Her destiny was a single room,
reached through a maze of outer rooms, the entrance to
which was guarded by a sliding bookcase and eight locking
doors, three of which required an electronic code to open
them. The chamber floor was uneven, the ventilation
system erratic, the air stale. It already had the smell of
decay that would never leave it. But five-star ratings were
not what Fritzl was after. Its ultimate purpose was as a
prison and, in that respect, the cellar passed muster.
Later Franz Polzer, the policeman charged with the most
unusual case he will ever deal with, would say of it:
'Already, in the planning phase, there was an intention to
add something within this regular building – something
unknown, something out of sight of the construction
authority, a small area, a little secret, a little dungeon.'

It was not unusual for homes in Lower Austria, teeter-

ing as they were on the edge of the Iron Curtain throughout the years of Europe's cold war, to have bunker-like
cellars with thick concrete and steel reinforced doors. In
1978, Josef Fritzl applied for permission from the planning board in Amstetten to build his bunker, and that is
how he always referred to it – not as a basement, nor a
cellar, but a bunker. In fact, he received a generous sub-
sidy amounting to the schilling equivalent of £2,000 when
the seal of approval was granted in 1983. The threat of a
nuclear war was real; the construction of bunkers was encouraged. Hermann Gruber, a spokesman for Amstetten
council, confirms that building inspectors scrutinized the
project in 1983 with an on-site visit and 'didn't notice
anything suspicious'. He adds his belief that, 'Mr Fritzl
had not stuck to the original plans but had secretly
expanded the cellar area.'

Indeed he had. But on the 1983 inspection visit, and
on a subsequent one carried out by the fire department,
no one noticed the sliding wall where the bookshelves
were situated and which hid the gangway to the cellar
complex. A third routine inspection by the fire department in 1999 would also fail to find it.

Local mayor Helmut Katzengruber says: 'As the local
planning authority we are responsible for licensing projects like this, but we had no idea of the extra rooms. We
have pored over documents, paperwork, statements from
a hundred tenants who lived at Ybbsstrasse 40 and dozens
of neighbours. Nobody had a clue what he'd done. There
is only one person who knows for sure – and he's in
prison. Whether he chooses to give an answer is the only
way we will ever find out.'

Fritzl constructed his bunker as an extension of the cellar that had been in the original house, built on the site in 1896. The authorities approved the outer rooms that Fritzl used as his work and storage spaces: a workroom proper, a utility room, two storerooms, a room for stacking wood to burn in the stove to heat the house and water supply, and two rooms for storing various spare parts as well as odds and ends. Unbeknown to the bureaucrats, carved from part of the old, small, damp and decrepit original basement, was the secret chamber where his master plan would begin. Using his skills as an electrician and builder he patiently worked at it every weekend for hours at a time, and often in the evening. Above ground, there was no hammering or drilling to be heard by neighbours or tenants. He was free to make as much noise as he liked. As was Elisabeth later.

The neighbour Danielczyk, who had witnessed the boy Josef being raised by his mother's fists, saw fleeting glances of him building this catacomb; snapshots which are now etched in her brain. Of course she had no idea what its ultimate purpose was to be; like everyone else, she had no inkling of the secret room beyond the wall. 'I remember there seemed to be a digger in the garden for ages. He was always wheelbarrowing earth out of the cellar entrance, then shovelling it into a skip in the garden. He shifted loads of earth – over 150 tons, I later read. I suppose if people had checked such things they'd have seen that there was more earth coming out of the place than the original plans would've calculated for. But no one did, did they?'

Although permission to build it was only granted in

1. A rare photograph that shows Josef Fritzl aged 16 (*circled*). A troubled childhood meant his schooling was delayed so that he was two years older than his classmates.

2. At this reunion picture, taken in 2006, old school pals congratulated Josef (*circled*) on his business success. His wife Rosemarie was as usual not allowed to attend, staying at home instead to attend to the children.

3. Detail from a school photo taken at the Polytechnische Lehrgang Amstetten. Elisabeth, then aged 15, is at the bottom of the photograph, her best friend Christa Woldrich above.

4. Elisabeth Fritzl, aged about 17, is pictured in the centre with her left hand clasped over her right wrist, looking straight at the camera. She is preparing for a wedding procession in her hometown of Amstetten.

5. Two of Elisabeth's sisters enjoyed this holiday in Italy with their mother. But Elisabeth was not allowed to go with them.

6. The ordinary-looking terraced house that the Fritzl family lived in, along with several tenants.

7. A policeman stands guard over the rear entrance to the Fritzls' house. Josef Fritzl used to carry wheelbarrows of food down the garden and through this entrance for his cellar family.

8. The expansive property possessed a roof terrace and over 66 rooms. The outside entrance to the cellar can be seen protruding from the rear wall of the house.

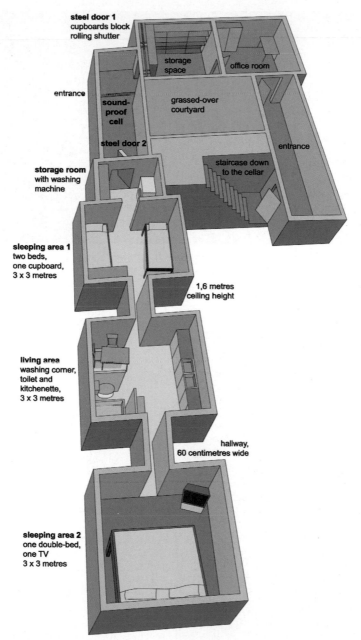

steel door 1
cupboards block
rolling shutter

storage
space

office room

entrance

**sound-
proof
cell**

grassed-over
courtyard

steel door 2

entrance

staircase down
to the cellar

storage room
with washing
machine

sleeping area 1
two beds,
one cupboard,
3 x 3 metres

1,6 metres
ceiling height

living area
washing corner,
toilet and
kitchenette,
3 x 3 metres

hallway,
60 centimetres wide

sleeping area 2
one double-bed,
one TV
3 x 3 metres

9. The layout of the hidden cellar, which was built in secret without the knowledge of the local authority.

10. The flat in the Fritzl house of tenant Alfred Dubanovsky. It was here he noticed a strange smell around the time the baby boy died in the cellar.

11. The cramped bathroom that Fritzl built for Elisabeth and her three children.

12. The narrow passageway leading to the sleeping area of the dungeon.

13. A corner of the dungeon that was under construction by Fritzl when his cellar family was discovered.

14. The Seestern guest house, which was owned by Josef Fritzl between 1973 and 1996 and was rebuilt after a fire gutted the building in 1982. The Fritzl family owned both this and a nearby campsite, and later Josef would enjoy summers there while Elisabeth was in her cellar.

15. The fire that destroyed the Seestern was caused by arson, and although police were convinced Josef Fritzl started the fire to pocket the insurance payout, charges against him were later dropped due to lack of evidence.

1983, it is accepted that Fritzl started work on the illegal section much sooner; he simply would not have had enough time to shift all the earth and get everything in working order in just 12 months. Like the supplies he would later purchase to keep the cellar dwellers alive, he bought the components of the dungeon at distant DIY stores and building depots. He used top-grade steel and concrete, some of it supplied at a discount through connections at the building firm he used to work for.

The hidden cellar had two access points: a hinged door that weighed 500kg, which became unusable over the years because of its weight, and a metal door, reinforced with concrete and on steel rails, which weighed 300kg and measured 1m high and 60cm wide. It was located behind a shelf in Fritzl's basement workshop and was protected by an electronic code known only to him, which he entered using a remote control unit. Eight doors had to be accessed to reach the chamber and all were custom-made. Five were equipped with an intricate locking system that required a special cylindrical key; two needed an electronic code to open them. The third and final gateway into the gloom beyond would also require an electronic code to open it, but that door would not be installed until Fritzl was ready for his tenant to move in – and the tenant would have to help him. The ultimate twist of the knife: Elisabeth would slot into place the last building brick of her own dungeon.

The bunker slotted perfectly into Fritzl's Nazi mindset. The regime he admired, and which had influenced him so much, was itself obsessed with underground bolt-holes, secret chambers, clandestine warrens. It was estimated that at the end of the war, for every metre of building above ground in the Nazi capitals of Berlin and Vienna, there were four metres underground. Places of sanctuary, of secrecy, where no one but the privileged elite were permitted to go. As with them, so with him. This was Fritzl's domain.

Viennese psychotherapist Kurt Kletzer believes that Fritzl's youthful admiration for the Nazis stayed with him throughout his life and that he may even have used it, in his own mind, as a justification for his actions. 'Josef Fritzl does not see a reality that the rest of us see. He tries to argue that, because he was born in very terrible times, his character, his ego, can be understood and, left unspoken, can also be forgiven. But out of the ruins of World War Two came people like Willy Brandt and the young Gerhard Schroeder and doctors, philosophers, poets, charity workers and Nobel Peace Prize winners. Blaming the times is a way out of a manipulator, a man who refuses to take responsibility for his actions. Fritzl allied his perverted lusts to an incredibly agile criminal mind. I do not think he was insane. I do think he was a very bad individual . . .

'It takes a mindset of incalculable cruelty to construct something like this and will go against his insanity defence because it was so clearly malice aforethought. The returns on this particular investment would not be accessible for years down the line. It shows an utter ruthlessness that was due, in part, to his sexual obsession, but also a compulsion to fool people, to "get away with" a crime in plain sight. A former work colleague of his called him a "borderline genius" and I believe he was, albeit a criminal one.'

In 1983, aged 17, Elisabeth moved over 300 kilometres away from home as part of her work as an apprentice waitress in a Tyrolean motel in Angath. Her friend and former colleague Heidi Stocker remembers an Elisabeth far removed from the shy, awkward Sissy of her school-days. Heidi, now 42, had first met Elisabeth when they were both 15, studying and working together on the apprenticeship programme. She got to know a girl whose character more closely resembled the 'wild child' her daddy was so set against.

'She was absolutely having the time of her life in the Tyrol. She was one of the wildest party girls I've ever met. She was always sneaking out the window of our dorm at night to meet up with boys – and then would stay out all night drinking, dancing and having fun. She wouldn't get back until the next day – and of course then there'd be all hell to pay, because she'd never be in a fit state to work.

'It was only teenage exuberance and high jinks. Sissy was a real scream to be around, the life and soul of the party – and absolutely the loveliest person you could meet. Everyone flocked around her like a moth to the flame. We nicknamed her Sissy because she was pretty, petite and doll-like, just like the Kaiserin Sissy of the old Austrian Habsburg family. But she was very naughty as well as very nice. She had a face like a china doll and looked as if butter wouldn't melt in her mouth – but she could down more beer, schnapps and wine than most.

She partied hard and worked as little as she could, and she used to drive our boss Franz Perner crazy with her moonlight flits and drunken antics.

'He was always a bit too touchy-feely with her and I know Sissy hated that. But she just had that kind of effect on men. In the end, Franz told her that if she sneaked out the window and went off on a crazy binge one more time, she'd be sacked and sent home. And then I'll never forget the sudden change in her. She burst into tears and started proper sobbing. She told me: "If they really send me home, I'll run away immediately because I can't stand being at home any more."

'I remember taking her in my arms to comfort her, patting her on the back and telling her: "There, there, it's going to be all right." But then I just didn't have a clue about the extent of the atrocities that were happening to her at home. I never even had a clue because Sissy always seemed such a happy, happy girl. Everyone loved her. She was really popular.

'I know that Sissy wanted to stay in Tyrol and finish her education there. But she needed her parents' permission to do that and her father refused to give it – and so she did eventually have to return home to him. Now I know why.'

Theresia Pfaffeneder, another friend who studied and worked with her in Strengberg, also knew Sissy to be 'high-spirited and fun'. Theresia recalls: 'She was the quintessential party girl out to have fun, and she never let anything get in the way of that.'

It was while she was studying at catering school in 1982 that Sissy also landed her first proper boyfriend and fell in love for the very first time. But her blossoming relationship with Andreas Kruzik – who was training to be a chef/waiter – only served to incense her possessive and warped father even more. In a letter to a pal written in May, 1984 – just three months before she was imprisoned in the secret dungeon – Sissy revealed: 'Andreas and I have been together since that course but, at the moment, we have some problems because he is from Enzesfeld-Lindabrunn and we are very far from each other, and that makes me sad.' She later confided that she was planning to leave home again shortly after her exams. She wrote to her friend: 'I'm moving in with my sister and her boyfriend. They can't afford the apartment – but for me it's cheap. I have two rooms on my own and I'm only paying seventy pounds a month.'

Her continued late-night partying, however, meant Sissy almost failed her final-year exams. She only just scraped through with five grade 4 passes – grade 5 being a fail. Her father was predictably furious. But the late-night benders weren't the only reason for Sissy's poor marks. As her father continued to abuse her, she confided to a friend (who asked not to be identified): 'I'm totally stressed. My nerves aren't the best any more.'

Fritzl knew the life Sissy was leading. He had to move fast. Independence was claiming his daughter from him; she had met a boy who loved her. This could not happen – he would not allow this to happen.

Andreas is married now, a father, aged 42 – the same age as the fresh-faced Sissy to whom he lost his heart all those years ago. She was the apprentice waitress, he the trainee cook. Love struck among the soup tureens and the stockpots when he spotted her at the tourism and catering school where Sissy studied two things – her trade, and how to avoid weekend trips home. 'I last saw her one month before she vanished,' says Andreas, the memory of Elisabeth vivid in his mind. 'I loved her, in a puppy love way. Your first love always stays with you in that way, doesn't it? She was a lovely girl. I fell for her the first time I saw her. She was pretty and fun, yet also serious and at times very withdrawn. Contemplative. When I expressed an interest in her she reciprocated pretty quickly.

'It was not so simple to be intimate because such things were not allowed in the school and there were only a few opportunities to make out. The girl's dormitory was a strict taboo and any boy who got caught there would have been expelled from the school. We were physically intimate, petting I suppose you would term it, but when I tried to take it further, she pulled back. I now know why.'

At that stage Elisabeth had endured sexual abuse, sexual torment, for seven long years. The ultimate act with a man was something repellent.

'We found somewhere to go – to, you know, be intimate – but we never made love. She spoke of her parents and her home only once, and said that she had a very strict father. She said he got her a waitress apprenticeship at a petrol station, but that she would've preferred to become a cosmetician.'

It is perhaps the ultimate tragedy of the whole Fritzl saga that Elisabeth went into the cellar as a virgin: not physically, but without knowing adult physical love as it should be shared, between willing partners who care for the feelings of, and the pleasure due to, one another. From her, sex was exacted, and would continue to be taken for more years than she will ever care to remember. That her father stole this from her is something that causes Andreas great anguish.

During her brief romance with Andreas the young lovers went to Vienna to see a show – *West Side Story* – which ironically has as its theme doomed love. And when their course finished Elisabeth got drunk – the behaviour that her father abhorred. 'Sissy had too much wine to drink and became all hyper. But at least we stayed together until the early hours of the morning,' Andreas remembers. The last time he saw Sissy was when her parents picked her up from the school to take her home in July, 1984 – just one month before her ordeal began. He was not allowed to say goodbye as Elisabeth climbed into her father's grey Mercedes, because she was banned from talking to boys.

'I wasn't allowed to see her off because her father wasn't supposed to see me. She would've been in trouble if he had.' But he did steal a kiss from her that morning. 'As we kissed goodbye, we promised each other to write as often as possible. But then I thought she'd lost interest in me. Now I realize she was no longer able to answer my letters.'

In the month before her disappearance, Elisabeth would write about her boyfriend Andreas to a friend, named only as Ernst, who also went to the same catering school. Ernst also came forward after seeing the news about her release. He says: 'It was a huge shock. I was terribly shaken, but also very angry and full of hate for her father. But now the media only paint a picture of Elisabeth as a victim. I'd like to show the world a different image of Elisabeth, as I knew her. She was a happy girl who enjoyed life and had plans for the future.

'I didn't know that she had been abused by her father. Now I think to myself: Why didn't she say anything? I've spent 24 years living a good life in freedom, and Sissy was locked up for all that time. That's not right. I hate her father very, very much. If I had a say, he'd get a much harder punishment than what he's facing today. Our laws are far too lax.'

In those last fleeting days and weeks of freedom, as Elisabeth made plans for a life without her father, she wrote letters to her friend Ernst. They would finally emerge many years later, time-warped missives tossed from a lifeboat headed for the bottom of a deep, dark sea, re-emerging to help paint a picture of the lively young lass whose life would be squandered underground. They break the heart of those who read them; for their joy, for their innocence, for the delight at being alive although, God knows, she hadn't had much to rejoice about during her upbringing. Sissy Fritzl's letters are a portal into a world of normal feelings and aspirations cruelly cut short. But the real world was already receding; the netherworld was beckoning.

The letters, signed 'Sissy' or just 'S', reflect her carefree attitude and day-to-day preoccupations, mirroring those of most teenagers her age: socializing, fashion, boyfriends, the weather, travel plans, sport. In the first of three letters she has been recovering from an illness and writes:

'Basically, I'm doing pretty well. Sometimes I still feel some pain, and feel sick.'

She tells her friend Ernst, who lived in Wiener Neustadt, that she was happy to receive a long letter from him. She was missing her boyfriend, Andreas, and writes about applying for a job in a nearby town, telling Ernst: 'Keep your fingers crossed for me! As soon as I've moved I'll send you my new address. You could come and visit me with your friends if you want to.' Then she describes her new haircut, which was 'layered on the sides and on the fringe. At the back I want to let it grow long.'

She writes about trust and describes her older brother fondly. She shows her affection for Ernst when she asks him: 'I have a sensitive question I want to ask. I'd like to know if we're going to stay friends when you have a girlfriend. Most of the time friendships break up because of that. And it's very important to me. If you can believe it, I deal with boys much better than girls. Girls aren't as trustworthy as boys. Probably that's because I've been around my brother since I was a little child. I'm very proud of my brother Harald, who is now 21 years old. I know his problems and he knows mine, and I wouldn't say anything bad about him.' She concludes by saying: 'I hope we see each other soon. Best regards.' She attaches a snap of herself by a swimming pool and adds: 'PS – the picture is a little bit dark, but I'll send you better ones soon, OK? And it's very important to me.'

One letter, written at night while she lay on her bed, is decorated with a cartoon girl dancing in a yellow dress. She discusses getting drunk and having several partygoers sleep the night at her flat. She writes: 'Hello, Ernst. It is now already half past ten and I'm lying in bed. Of course I went out on Saturday. Can you imagine how hammered I was? At first we went to a couple of clubs. At about 5 a.m. we all went to my place to get a coffee because we'd had so much fun, and they all slept at my place. That was a mess. It took me half a day to clean up the flat.' The young Elisabeth's love of binge-drinking was something her father would later claim was one of the main reasons why he devised his plan to lock her away.

Elisabeth also writes of her new job and enjoying swimming and tennis on her days off. She describes her brothers and sisters and says she likes 'listening to music and daydreaming'; she calls her clubbing pals her 'crew'. Elisabeth ends one letter by saying: 'Stay safe, keep being a good boy. Don't drink too much.' And another: 'I hope you keep your promise that you'll visit me as soon as you get your driving licence.'

The final letter reveals plans which were never fulfilled because her father locked her away in the underground dungeon. She writes of her stress at upcoming exams and enjoying the film she was watching while writing the letter. Her last words to her friend before her 24 years of imprisonment were: 'Bye, see you soon, S. Write back soon and don't get drunk for no reason! Think of me!'

Think of me. People could think what they liked, as far as Fritzl was concerned – his thoughts were concentrated on getting his prize underground as soon as possible.

Elisabeth moved back to the house for the summer as she made her plans for an independent life. Unfortunately, her plans would be steamrollered by her father's. With contacts in all sorts of places, at some point during the previous month Fritzl had laid his hands on a litre bottle of ether; clear, odourless, highly inflammable and, if used properly, extremely effective in knocking someone out. Still used in some developing countries as an anaesthetic, Fritzl stored it in a brown glass jar in one of his cellar workrooms.

What happened during the day of August 28 remains unclear; Elisabeth testified about it in her videotaped statement to police in July, 2008 – and details of it will emerge at Fritzl's trial. From police insiders it seems that Fritzl asked Elisabeth to go with him into the cellar 'to help me fix something'. This was an invitation that must have been scary, to say the least. She had been abused by him for years and now he wanted her to go to the domain that had always been so strictly out of bounds to all – tenants and family alike.

She trod the 11 steps to the bunker for the first – and last – time, took her last breaths as a free woman. That morning, unknown to her, was the last time she would put make-up on in her bedroom mirror, the last time she would brush her teeth in the family bathroom, the last day she would make plans. Her life was on the cusp of being airbrushed from history.

Fritzl said he needed her to help put a door in place. He led her through the warren of the illicit cellar – but how would she distinguish the secret and illegal from what had been authorized and allowed? He led her one by one through the maze of doors that would seal her fate and muffle her cries, until they came to the last door. The heavy one he required her to hold in place while he calibrated it into its frame.

What did she think, as she gazed through the murk into the corridor that led to the room? That he was equipping the house with a new utility room for the tenants to use? Her mother, perhaps? At some point the door was in place, she dusted herself off to go, and a hand containing a towel soaked in some kind of alcohol was clasped across her face. She struggled but felt nauseous . . . then weak . . . then nothing.

Goodbye, Sissy.

5. A Sort of Life

Before the children, there were only terror and boredom as companions in her lost world. Afterwards, at least, Elisabeth had a diversion; she had to stay strong for them. She summoned up resources of courage and fortitude to survive in a situation that would have broken stronger individuals than her many times over. But for close to the first five years of her internment in that evil-smelling, mouldy, silent world, she lived without conversation, without books, often without even a sense of time. She could not even hear the footfalls of her tormentor as he walked down the 11 steps that separated her world from his, because of the thickness of the walls and the concrete door. Day was night and night was day, a hazy blur of infinitely slow hours melding into one excruciating mass of wasted life, encroaching like a fungus on her soul. She kept no journal, had no one to turn to, had no one to hear her cries – except God. She prayed constantly that he would save her, her pleas taking on a meaning and a depth impossible for her to imagine in the days when she used to attend Sunday Mass regularly with her mother, brothers and sisters. Only Josef had stayed away from church, and yet now it was he alone who would hear her prayers for 24 long years – and ignore them.

Her first revelations show the depth of her despair. In those first days and hours Elisabeth banged on the walls and clawed at the ceiling, howling in pain and anguish for help that would not come. She broke her fingernails and clawed away the skin until blood was dripping down her forearms. She made herself sick through screaming; she cried until she didn't have any tears left. She didn't know a person could cry as much as she did.

She had no way of knowing that eight separate doors guarded this labyrinth – the last weighing half a ton, the one she had helped put in place. A bomb could quite literally go off in the cellar and no one walking outside the house would have heard it. Which is exactly the way her father had meticulously planned it.

She controlled nothing. Only the time she could go to the toilet or wash. She paced around the labyrinth like some demented Minotaur, seeking an exit that wasn't there. And she would try to lose herself in her past – a past that contained little of pleasure with its beatings and its secretive nocturnal visits by her abusive father – trying desperately to recall some moments of joy. She would imagine games played in the meadows behind the Seestern in the summer months when her father was away in some foreign country, or in Amstetten, and she had been free from his tyranny. She remembered the kindnesses of her mother: the money scrimped to buy her presents that Josef never approved of or allowed; swimming in the Mondsee; going off with her sisters to meet friends on the campsite. The friends she had started to make as she prepared to break away like her older siblings.

Some days she would pretend she was on a hiking holiday. She would pick a distant mountain spot she had been to in her childhood, plot in her mind how long it would take to walk to it, and set off. She would have the lights off as she paced the length of the 35-square-metre dungeon, because she knew the number of steps by heart. After two hours she would switch the strip lighting on, pretend that a bright dawn had come up and was reflecting the snow-capped peaks on to a lake that existed nowhere except in her mind. She would walk for hours around the room, then pick up sandwiches made earlier, pausing on a bed to eat them, pretending she was on a rock watching squirrels scamper up a large fir tree. Then she would try to sleep for an hour, pretending the soft rays of the sun were washing across her face, the white clouds scudding by in a blue sky. As she drifted off she would hum the strains of an old carol 'Still, Still, Still' that Austrians traditionally sing as a lullaby. Her mother used to sing it to her and her siblings when she was young.

> Still, still, still,
> One can hear the falling snow.
> For all is hushed,
> The world is sleeping,
> Holy Star its vigil keeping.
> Still, still, still,
> One can hear the falling snow.
>
> Sleep, sleep, sleep,
> 'Tis the eve of our Saviour's birth.
> The night is peaceful all around you,
> Close your eyes,
> Let sleep surround you.

Sleep, sleep, sleep,
'Tis the eve of our Saviour's birth.

Dream, dream, dream,
Of the joyous day to come.
While guardian angels without number
Watch you as you sweetly slumber.
Dream, dream, dream,
Of the joyous day to come.

She would wake up, the faint whirr of the refrigerator and the metallic buzz of the strip lighting the only sounds. If the fantasy was still strong, still vibrant, so real she could almost taste the pine-scented air of the mountains, she would continue her 'hike'. More often than not, she would collapse in tears, remembering her first day in this concrete coffin, how she had begged her father not to do this to her. Elisabeth felt her father had gone mad. She begged him not to do this. She promised she would be anything he wanted her to be if he would only not do this to her.

She was hyperventilating as she looked into his pitiless grey-green eyes, the eyes of a tyrant. She felt as if her chest would collapse inwards, felt the veins in her neck bulging. She swallowed the bile that rose in her throat, gagging in her frenzy of tears and desperation. She and her school friends nicknamed her father 'Dracula' behind his back, the moniker earned from a combination of his love for dark clothes, his unfortunate hairstyle and his piercing eyes – dead eyes, some called them.

'It's too late for you, Liesl,' he said, in his clipped nasal

Austrian dialect. 'You have defied me for much too long. You are wicked, now you must pay.' His wrath was almost Biblical in its dimensions, payback for what he viewed as a licentious lifestyle at odds with his own personal code. All the secretive elements of his character melded together and crystallized in this underground kingdom of which he was the supreme master. The omnipotence he felt was a large component of the sexual frisson he experienced simply by locking up this daughter who had been destined for so long to become his secret concubine.

Elisabeth would rewind her mental video recorder endlessly to replay the horror of that first day and the life she had left behind. She remembered her upbringing in the house, what she told her school friends was a 'life on tiptoes'. She joked that, 'We could all have been ballet dancers. We could walk through a minefield, we were that nimble on our feet when he was around.' The compulsion that Josef Fritzl had to control, to dominate, made her formative years a miserable time, one which she would be able to look back on with little joy. Her mother had loved her, certainly, her brother Harald and rebellious Rosie, and little Doris. But Harald and Rosie were already gone, and she had been on the verge of following them when her tormentor came for her one last time to commit her to the unendurable. And yet she had to endure.

It was on 28 August, 1984, that she was kidnapped and forced to live in this hell. The clock stopped on a day when the Austrian government decided to pay subsidies for teenagers without jobs, when British ports were hit with a strike by dockers, when American pop icon Frank Zappa announced he would come to Austria in the autumn for a concert she would never see, when former Wimbledon champion Björn Borg announced he wasn't the father of his girlfriend's baby, and when the trial began in Hamburg of the forger of the 'Hitler diaries' who conned a world Elisabeth would part company from for the biggest part of her life.

Stuart Grassian, an American psychiatrist, has explored in depth the effects of prolonged solitary confinement upon individuals within the American penal system – itself no longer immune from charges of intolerance and inhumanity. Yet at least the residents of US jails are there because they've done something wrong – and the sentences are usually finite. Elisabeth was confined simply for being herself. And there was to be no parole.

Dr Grassian, on the faculty of the Harvard Medical School since 1974, recognizes that inmates confined alone – captives who had as much and, in some cases, more mental stimuli than Elisabeth – were soon placed in danger of suffering severe psychiatric harm. This harm includes a specific syndrome which has been reported by many clinicians in a variety of settings, 'all of which have in common features of inadequate, noxious and restricted environmental and social stimulation. In more severe cases, this syndrome is associated with agitation, self-destructive behaviour, and overt psychotic disorganization. In addition, solitary confinement often results in severe exacerbation of a previously existing mental condition, or in the appearance of a mental illness where none had been observed before. Even among inmates who do not develop overt psychiatric illness as a result of confinement in solitary, such confinement almost inevitably imposes significant psychological pain during the period of isolated confinement.'

He notes that many of the acute symptoms suffered by these inmates are likely to subside upon termination of solitary confinement, but also that many other inmates – including some who did not become overtly psychiatrically ill during their confinement in solitary – would likely suffer permanent harm as a result of such confinement. This harm is most commonly manifested by a continued intolerance of social interaction, a handicap which 'often severely impairs the inmate's capacity to reintegrate into the broader community upon release from imprisonment'. Translation: ultimately freedom may prove to be no freedom at all.

Elisabeth heard voices in the cellar – something else that she shared with the long-term victims of cruel prison regimes. She suffered illusions, and hallucinations, whispered voices saying frightening things, such as foretelling a violent death. She suffered agonizing images of food that was not available to her: great weighted trays of pancakes and stuffed beef rolls; her mother's Wiener schnitzels pounded paper thin and topped with fried eggs; red cabbage braised in beef stock and wine. She loved her mother's cooking and the memories of it tormented her. These were vistas like the false oases that desert survivors see when the water is running low and the sun is beating down. She could almost taste the food – but of course she never would.

Fritzl kept her fridge-freezer stocked with cheap, chemically infused TV dinners, inexpensive cuts of meat, frozen precooked vegetables, ice cream and oven chips.

Little wonder that later in her confinement her teeth
would fall out like acorns dropping from oak trees and
she would develop a form of scurvy, the sort that used
to afflict British sailors in Victorian times with little or no
access to fresh fruits.

She had visions whereby the objects in the cellar – the
beds, the cooker, the fridge – grew larger or smaller as
she stared at them. Sometimes, they even seemed to melt
in front of her eyes. Confusion and bewilderment created
their own perfect psychiatric storms. She would, on
occasions, 'trash' the cellar, tearing up food wrappings,
flinging bed sheets to the ground, ripping up towels, even
swamping the floor with water. But each act of rebellion
cost her dearly at the hands of her jailer. She was beaten
and she was verbally abused on many occasions as he strove
to grind disobedience out of her soul with an iron fist.

Amid the delirium-like states, as she paced like a caged
tiger in her oppressive captivity, were fearful dreams of
vengeance. She dreamed of burning her father alive, of
poking his eyes out with spears, of mutilating him in ways
that she didn't know she knew of.

'Human beings are naturally curious,' says psychology
expert Carly Frintner. 'Drastically reducing the amount
of normal social interaction, of reasonable mental stimu-
lus, of exposure to the natural world, of almost everything
that makes life human and bearable, is emotionally, physically and psychologically destructive – because it denies
us the ability to ask questions and seek reasons and
information, to form explanations that allow us to understand ourselves as well as our world and our place and
purpose in the world. It is logical that we feel less stable

and secure overall when the things that our brain and body rely on to connect to and understand our surroundings are taken away from us.'

Terrible though her imprisonment was, the will to live was stronger than the desire to die. Elisabeth was 18 with a head full of dreams and desires. By degrees they were lost, as her spirit and dignity were cruelly degraded and broken by the man who was supposed to love her with all his heart as a father. Yet she somehow found the resources to carry on living.

The tedium was excruciating but, after several months, a routine developed that she hoped would give her some purpose. She tried to live like a citizen of the world she had left behind – sleeping at night, as dictated by the clock, and staying awake during daylight hours. She would rise at 8 a.m. and have some breakfast of cereal and toast. She would eat it wrapped in a blanket; for the first few years the cellar was primitive before Fritzl began both expanding it and making it more comfortable, such as providing electric fan heaters. After breakfast she would either 'hike' around the dungeon or try to meditate on happier things. She made a mental list of all the places she wanted to visit in the world including New York, Paris and London. Afterwards she would shower and make herself a frozen pizza or cutlet from the supplies that her captor brought down to her once every three to five days. Then she would sleep, awake to the living nightmare, and the whole process would repeat itself.

She soon noticed that she was short of breath on her 'hikes' around the cellar and put it down to a lack of proper exercise. In fact she was suffering from a shortage of oxygen, a problem that would be exacerbated when the children came. Fritzl had gone to great lengths to make his lair habitable, secret and well ventilated. It was certainly secret, but barely habitable and most certainly not well ventilated. A weak electric fan funnelled in air from a pipe with twists and turns. The air was stale and acrid before it seeped into the cellar. There was also no system to take out the CO_2 produced by Elisabeth's body in the simple act of breathing. Over time she noticed mildew forming on the tiling, in the narrow corridor between the rooms, around the taps and the shower head. The walls felt damp to the touch and the tiling shimmered with a glossy sheen. Water droplets formed on the wood panelling roof near to the shower area. Slowly but surely, Elisabeth's breathing began to deteriorate and a healthy young woman suddenly began developing bronchial problems. But this was just the beginning of Elisabeth Fritzl's martyrdom.

Fritzl has said that he did not begin assaulting Elisabeth until 1985, one full year after she was secreted in the dungeon. Given that he is a manipulative and corrupt personality capable of pulling off the vast charade of telling the world that his daughter had run away to join a bizarre sect, yet all the while imprisoning her, the veracity of his claim cannot be gauged. In her statement to the police she said that he began abusing her when she was 11, something he denies, but again – how much credence can be given to a man who went on to treat his daughter like a sex slave? Appropriate boundaries between them were blurred and then obliterated when she was a child, as Elisabeth realized she was living to meet his needs instead of her own. She told her friends so; it would seem they have no reason to lie in recounting what she said all those years ago, before she disappeared. So while it remains unclear exactly when the sexual abuse in the cellar began, begin it most certainly did.

He came for her in that chill, windowless warren, and he raped her. A man whose appetites stretched to prostitutes and pornography was exacting what he came to regard as his 'due'. What Elisabeth thought when he arrived that first time without supplies, but with a demand for sex, we will probably never know. Yet his violation of her added a new and even more terrifying element to her incarceration. She had no contraception and she was not an ignorant young woman; she knew that the risks of pregnancy, and of a child being born with genetic defects, were high. She had excelled in biology classes at school, and she understood the risks she was being exposed to by her father – yet she was powerless against him. She could only acquiesce or suffer fearful beatings at his hands as he hurled insult upon insult down in tandem with his fists.

Day or night, it didn't matter to Elisabeth; every day was the same for her. A rhythm developed, a pattern whereby her father would show up virtually every three days to vent his lust upon her. In his ordered but deeply disturbed mind, Josef Fritzl rewarded his daughter's innate fear of him with 'treats' intended to improve her quality of life in the dungeon. He provided some mats. He brought in a radio. He installed a TV and a video recorder, gave her a heater. These, like the food and the sanitary items Elisabeth needed, were bought in shops far away from Fritzl's home, away from anyone who might recognize him and become suspicious about his purchases. This was the pattern that he had established, and was to repeat successfully for many years to come.

In a grotesque parody of normality he began to sit with his daughter, engaging her in conversation. 'This is nice and cosy, isn't it?' he would say, pouring himself a beer, showing her photographs from his latest holiday or gossiping about the neighbours who were lost to her for ever. He told her of the roof garden he had built on top of the house, where he had planted kohlrabi and swede, leeks and carrots. (He had to make his garden there; the foundations of the cellar were too near the surface to allow him to cultivate at ground level.) He told her what was on TV, what was happening with the rest of the family, how her siblings were faring. The savage pain she felt as she was forced to listen to tales of the real world just metres above her head – hearing what was happening in the place her father had chosen to isolate her from – can only be guessed at. Her own vision and expectations were degraded along with her spirit until she reached the point where the conversations were actually something she looked forward to, because they spelled a brief respite from her lonely incarceration.

As a child she had been inherently helpless and subordinate, a state which Fritzl liked and encouraged; consequently, when she began to display independence, to move away from his orbit of influence, he had to act and the cellar was the appalling end station of his reasoning.

Doctors treating Elisabeth so many years after her

ordeal began recognize the symptoms of dissociation at work, a term which psychiatrists use to describe a state which abuse victims fall into while the abuse itself is occurring. It is a feeling of the body and mind separating.

Behavioural therapist and trauma expert Georg Pieper has treated victims of some of the worst accidents in Europe: survivors of the Eschede train crash in which over 100 people died; those who lived through the Erfurt school shootings of 2002 which took 19 lives; and the victims of a terrible mine accident in Borken. He is convinced Elisabeth survived for so long because of her ability to dissociate herself from the abuse, saying: 'By doing this she protected her mind from the impression that she could not cope.'

And so it went on, this life in quicksand. As Communism collapsed in the real world and mobile telephone technology was linking her friends in ways she could only dream about, Elisabeth Fritzl remained marooned in her concrete wilderness. Her skin became the colour of yellowing parchment. One day she looked in the mirror at her gums, fiddled with a tooth that had been giving her some pain, and it came out in her hand. The lack of vitamins in her diet led to chronic gingivitis which, in time, would claim most of her teeth. She had no access to fresh fruit, hardly ever ate fresh vegetables and as a result suffered a chronic lack of vitamins A, C, D and E, exacerbating her tooth decay. She hoped at one point that looking like a witch might have put her father off. It didn't.

All the while, above her, the suspicions of some people were growing, but no one ever managed to join up the dots, to make the connections that might have saved her sooner. One man who will regret this for the rest of his life is Sepp Leitner, the nightclub manager and former resident of the Ybbsstrasse house, who had his own niggling suspicions about his landlord. He lived in the flat directly over the cellar lair. Leitner's relationship with Fritzl was not good at the end, but Leitner admitted that at the beginning he thought he was OK. 'Just before he kicked me out I got a dog called Sam – Fritzl never liked him, but then my wife and I didn't like Fritzl. She used to call him the devil because of the way he looked. Interesting – Don't you think? – given that when he was finally banged up the other prisoners immediately called him Satan.

'I think he took against Sam because Sam *knew* in that instinctive way that animals have that something was not right in that house. The dog behaved strangely at all times. He wouldn't bark out the window or stand at the door . . . but he would lie on the floor, right over that cellar, and whine and whimper, looking quizzically at the floor as if trying to figure out something that was puzzling him. My wife used to joke that there were ghosts in the house, but I never had an explanation at the time. All I know is that a dog reacts in the direction he hears a noise; if he hears a noise from the side he barks to the side, if he hears a noise from outside he will bark outside, but if it comes from underground – well – that would explain why he stayed lying down and growled. I grew up with dogs and I know very well the way they work. And Fritzl did too; he wanted Sam gone because Sam was a threat, I see that now.

'Another thing was a lot of jiggery-pokery with the

electricity. I got an additional bill for 5,000 schillings [around £250] one year and I thought this was crazy. The flat wasn't even 30 square metres big, and didn't even have a washing machine in it. I used to do all my washing at my mother's. We rarely used the kitchen; we used to eat out all the time.

'A sparky friend came round to install cable television for me. He looked at the bill and said: "Something fishy here, Sepp." So we went around the flat together and turned every electrical appliance off, including the TV and even an alarm clock radio. Absolutely everything. And yet the electricity meter was still whirling around like a dervish! My friend told me to go to the council. My mistake was that I didn't do that, but I confronted Fritzl instead. "Something's up here," I said. "You're running stuff on my meter." That was it – we had a row and he gave me notice to quit. He changed the locks. If I'd only gone to the council and they'd tried to find where the electricity was going, maybe they might have uncovered this a lot sooner.

'People ask me what life was like living there, and when you put it all together it does create a strange picture, although at the time I didn't connect everything up. Fritzl was hated in the neighbourhood, but could anyone really believe he had created another world of torture for his own daughter?

'But I will have to live with my mistakes and it haunts me that I might have saved her. I remember one old geezer who I used to see sitting on his step at night when I came home from work. "How's the arsehole?" he'd ask. "Get your dog to bite him." In conversation with him one day he told me Fritzl was a convicted rapist, dragged out a faded old yellow press cutting to prove it too. I can't understand why everyone later said they didn't know about it.

'I had a bit of notice period before I had to go and so I threw a party for friends. It could only be a few people, there wasn't that much room. We played some music and, sure enough, before long he was at the door, demanding we turn down the noise. He came inside the flat and was shouting and my dog growled at him and he made as if to kick Sam. I was really annoyed and I wanted to hit him but my friends held me back. Fritzl accused me of being a drug addict and said he was going to call the police, but he never did. I guess it's obvious now that he wanted to avoid any trouble with the police.

'He also stole food from the fridges of other tenants. Now we know it was to supplement supplies in his secret dungeon. One of them told me how he came home early from work one day and spotted Fritzl coming out of his front door with a carton of milk in his hand. He said: "Hey, man, what the hell are you doing in my flat?" Fritzl stammered something about running out of milk and wanting to borrow some and how he was going to put it back. The other tenant was really annoyed. "This is my private flat," he told him. Fritzl offered to give him a reduction on his rent and promised it wouldn't happen again. But it became the talk of the house and got everyone thinking about the times they'd missed stuff – someone said he missed sausages in his fridge and I clearly remember missing a packet of noodles. The old bastard was raiding our cupboards at night or when we were out.

He was a genius at electrics and building a secret cave but clearly he got his shopping expeditions mixed up and needed to supplement them.'

Dubanovsky, Elisabeth's former school friend, also curses the benefits of hindsight. A tenant for 12 years, only now can he look at the clues and kick himself for not solving the riddle of her sudden disappearance. 'Now I think back on it, I suppose I should've wondered why he went down to the cellar every day,' he says. 'At the time I was like every other Austrian – none of my business, don't get involved. But he was a creepy guy, a secretive sort of guy. When I saw him carrying food down into the basement I thought back to my childhood, how my parents stored food in their cellar. So it didn't seem too weird to me when I saw him in the garden, carrying lots of stuff he'd just taken out of his car.

'I'm one hundred per cent sure that I heard some noises coming from the cellar. I actually asked what was going on in the cellar just under my flat, and Fritzl explained that it was the heating system that he'd just renewed and was "making some strange noises". He made the cellar a no-go zone. He didn't even want us to look out the windows into the garden. He said that this is "none of your business". There was always, too, some noise made by extractor fans. I've never been able to tell where they were placed. I know that every single flat had one, but an extractor fan was switched on all the time, day and night. I never thought that it was possible this noise came from downstairs, but when I think about it now, that seems logical.

'I also remember him complaining that he didn't want

anybody to take photographs of the house, the courtyard or the garden. I remember discussing it with him and telling him that nobody would probably want to take a photograph of those things anyway, and he replied: "You wait and see. One day this house will make history."'

Strange noises, mad electricity meters, whining hounds, suspicious residents and missing food. None of it mattered and Elisabeth continued her slow, inexorable, mental and physical decline. Lack of proper vitamins took its toll on her body in other ways. She experienced tingling in her fingers and toes, confusion, difficulty in maintaining balance, loss of appetite, exhaustion and weakened powers of concentration – the classic symptoms of a deficit of vitamin B1. The lack of vitamin B6 translated into skin inflammations and rashes, and her gums bled on an almost daily basis through lack of vitamin C. All the while she was breathing in the unhealthy air of the chamber, stooping more and more as she moved around, wheezing like an old hag in outdated clothes that Fritzl bought for her at cheap outlets far from home.

And then, in 1988, after nearly five years – which could have been fifteen or one as far as her time keeping went – Elisabeth missed her period. She knew what this meant. For Fritzl, it was what he dreamed of, the seed corn of a new, secret family, one which he alone would nurture in the half-light. Elisabeth told him that she was pregnant and that she would need to go to hospital and have proper medical care. Fritzl thought she was trying it on: she would have the child in the cellar.

He took the decisions, as he took all the decisions, and her confinement assumed a new dimension of horror as the birthing day approached. In his trusted E-class Mercedes he embarked on new shopping trips. In Linz, at a second-hand bookshop, he bought two 1960s books on childbirth and midwifery. He purchased nappies, towels, a plastic bowl, stainless-steel scissors, bandages, antiseptic wipes, disinfectant and his cure-all for ailments – aspirin. There were to be no epidurals for Elisabeth if the birth went badly. Elisabeth would have the baby alone in the darkness.

The word of law. The word of potential life and death.

With her belly growing larger by the day, and her anxieties along with it, Fritzl also laid in supplies of powdered milk and baby food and even bought a rattle with bright flowers on it. If he ever saw the irony in bringing such objects of the mundane into his under-world, he never displayed it.

Home birthing is not a new concept for many women in the world; in western societies in recent years it has taken on something of a social cachet for a woman to say she had a child at home, without the need for medical intervention. But that is a lifestyle choice, usually taken on the back of enormous pre-natal care, guidance and nutrition with a partner or medical expert close at hand if things go awry. There was no such luxury for Elisabeth. Alone, frightened, and weak from her poor diet, Elisabeth Fritzl brought Kerstin into the world nearly five years after she disappeared underground. A thing of tender, fragile beauty, in a shrunken universe that dripped water and stank of decay; the contrast was stunning.

The child slept at first in a cardboard box that Fritzl provided for her. However unwanted, the child was not unloved when she arrived. Elisabeth was a sweet-natured girl who had longed for her own family when she was growing up in the world beyond the concrete prison. She knew it was not the fault of this poor mite to be born into this pit of despair. And so, at last, she had a reason to get up and a reason to stay awake and a purpose not to die in the night which, before, had often seemed an easy and painless way out of her torture. Later, when it was all over, doctors would say that Elisabeth's courageous mothering instincts saved her and her children. She provided the cuddles and kisses, the cooing and aahing. She cooked the food, cleaned her daughter, bathed her and sang to her, just like her own mother used to sing to her. The lullabies were stored in her head; she repeated them now for a grandchild she thought Rosemarie would never see. The maternal instincts kicked in, exactly like the manipulative Fritzl knew they would, and he was completely satisfied with the way his scheme was taking shape.

In an interview for this book Wolfgang Bergmann, the head of the Institute for Child Psychology in Hanover, describes Elisabeth as 'a true heroine', one who saved herself and her children due to her deep-rooted maternal instincts. 'She survived through and for her offspring. The strength of a mother's love is best illustrated in extremis. What this woman endured is unbelievable . . . unbelievable. She brought the children alone into this world, nourished them and brought them up. Finally, she was able to bring them out of this hell.

'The children would have seen Josef Fritzl as a father figure even if they were told to call him grandfather. The relationship was plagued by strife; on the one hand he was the one who organized food and clothing, on the other he oversaw a brutal and threatening regime that kept them imprisoned, one in which threats were an everyday event.

'The deficits for the children alone in terms of "normality" are enormous. They had no social interaction with their peers. They will be extremely mistrustful to an incalculable extent. They have no experience themselves to draw on because they had no shared experiences with others. This lack of interaction shrank their ability to speak properly, to understand properly. They will have difficulty in remaining focused on things, will have trouble learning.

'The fact that there was a television there and it was playing a lot doesn't mean much. It might have been a distraction and a source of entertainment but it always described a world they had never known and therefore couldn't understand. It's all very well seeing leaves rustling in a wood, but you have to have been in a wood with rustling leaves to understand that. A television is no substitute for a real world.'

Waste and its disposal became a further problem in captivity. The smell of soiled nappies, decaying food, the toilet and the generally bad air were virtually intolerable on some days. Fritzl bought larger plastic sacks and ordered Elisabeth to be 'better organized' in making sure they were securely tied. Whatever he couldn't burn he would move out in the middle of the night to avoid detection from neighbours, dragging rubbish back through the secret door, leaving new supplies behind.

After Kerstin came Stefan in 1990 and Lisa in 1992. It was after Lisa's birth that Fritzl extended the cellar into two more rooms. By the time the police opened the final door to the last of the secret rooms, they found that the house at Ybbsstrasse 40 had a total of 66 rooms – including the secret cellar rooms. He beavered away like some troglodyte gold miner in a fairy tale, his shirt off and his muscles gleaming in the neon light as he hacked through walls to a cellar beyond, the residue of a previous house on the site, which he knew was there and could be utilized to extend his underground kingdom. Elisabeth was enlisted to help him in his renovations; the jailbird prolonging her own agonies by assisting her captor.

It was after the renovations that Fritzl came to Elisabeth with the news that he had decided to bring Lisa up with his wife. He expected her to rail against him, was prepared to beat her if she raised her voice to him. 'It will give you more room,' he said. But Elisabeth couldn't agree more. Although it went against the grain of her mothering instincts, in surrendering her baby daughter she was giving her a chance of a proper life, such as she had once known. She loved the company of her children and despised the life they were forced to lead in the cellar. Inevitably she would miss Lisa but any mother would take solace in the fact that she would go to school, get an education, fall in love; the basics of a normal existence denied to her and the other children.

The child was taken away from her. On 19 May, 1993, aged nine months, Lisa Fritzl felt natural light on her face for the first time as she was 'abandoned' by her mother on the doorstep of Fritzl's home upstairs. It was not a moment too soon – the child needed urgent medical care, a heart operation included, before she was able to be returned to Ybbsstrasse 40. All the time Rosemarie visited her, waited by her tiny cot and watched the tubes and drips feeding into her tiny form – prayed for her to survive. And she did.

The same escape was provided to daughter Monika, born in 1994. Elisabeth was desperate for her father to give the children to their grandmother, for them to grow up and enjoy a life they could never begin to imagine if they stayed with their mother in her underground world.

Then came twins Alexander and Michael, born in 1996. Michael died after three days, probably a victim of respiratory difficulties. Elisabeth, Stefan and Kerstin, marooned and illimitably sad, would have had to watch helplessly as the tiny infant died. Then they watched as Fritzl gathered his son up in one of the rubbish sacks and dragged him away as if he was so much rubbish. He told police later that he burned Michael's body in the heating incinerator of the house.

What happened to baby Michael could well decide whether Fritzl faces a murder charge with a mandatory sentence of life imprisonment if found guilty. At the time of writing prosecutors are poring over the Austrian legal code to determine whether his blatant neglect of the child's welfare amounts to murder precisely because he denied the baby the proper medical attention. Statements will have to come from Elisabeth, Stefan and Kerstin, the witnesses to Michael's birth and death. Elisabeth has told how, weak from the effort of a double birth, aided only by 7-year-old Kerstin and 6-year-old Stefan, she tried to keep her twin boys alive. How her father left her alone for three days as she pored over the medical books for something that might help her ailing son. How, by the time her father finally turned up, Michael had died.

Prosecutors will also interview Mr Dubanovsky who, while not a visual witness to Michael's death, believes he smelled the stench of the callous funeral which was arranged for the baby. 'I remember one time several years ago when I came home and there was this horrible smell everywhere inside the house. I wondered what this could be; I'd never smelled something similar before. There was just this one time that this happened and the smell was gone after a couple of days. Everybody knows that there can be strange smells when you throw something into an oven that's not supposed to be put there. That's why some friends of mine who came to visit made jokes with me about Fritzl heating the place with dead dogs and so on, instead of wood. Now I'm convinced that this smell must have been the dead baby's body he burned in the oven. I've told the police; the dates tally. I smelled this poor child being cremated without a prayer or a hymn. That's the work of the devil, if you ask me.'

The family suffered and supported one another in the intervals before Fritzl came to the cavern, listened while he ate with them and told them stories of his life above and the siblings whose birth they had witnessed, but whom they thought they would never see again. They celebrated the feast of Christmas together, and New Year, and all the promises for a new beginning and hope that the various festivals brought. Confusion is too small a word to describe what they must have felt.

Elisabeth procured paper and pens from Fritzl and taught the children to read and write. It is known that the children devoured nursery books and colouring books, and Fritzl brought them a basic multiplication textbook so Elisabeth was able to teach them the fundamentals of mathematics. In this extraordinary situation any mother would have had a stark choice to make: to tell her children the truth of what had happened to her, or to make up a story that they could share in, and so be less curious about the world they had never seen. Elisabeth chose the latter option. This meant turning reality on its head to fit their reality; she told them that the programmes they saw on the old Grundig TV set were a fantasy, that the stories of pirates and princesses she related were also a fantasy, that nothing was real in the outside world from which Fritzl emerged, and to which he returned after each visit. This was real, the only place that was safe, and 'grand-father' – Fritzl insisted his incestuous, illegitimate off-spring address him thus – was really keeping them safe.

Elisabeth used the little kitchen table, positioned next to the lavatory in the kitchen, as her schoolroom. She taught Stefan and Kerstin together, although her own academic knowledge was limited. Using a programme they had seen on TV as the basis for a lesson, she would ask the children to write about the woods they had seen on a nature programme, or the sea, or birds. These must have been alien, strange things for children who had never experienced them.

Elisabeth made sure they washed and dressed each day. She made sure they brushed their teeth but could do nothing to stop the decay brought on by the poor-quality food and lack of vitamins. She made Fritzl bring little presents – chocolates, key-ring toys – which she placed under their pillows each time another tooth fell out. There were lots of little toys under their pillows.

It is unknown what Fritzl told the children about his world. Elisabeth instructed them to respect him. Yet children being children cannot be programmed to obey at all times. They must have asked to go outside, if only for a short period, to see the things that others took for granted. The denials he gave them, together with his justification for them, have yet to be revealed.

The outside was forbidden yet it seeped through the concrete of the bunker to penetrate into their very souls. One day Elisabeth set the children a task of 'decorating' their home with brightly coloured posters. Kerstin and Stefan drew trees and fruit, fish and flowers. The world was beyond their reach so they had to create one. Seeing their efforts must have broken Elisabeth's heart yet filled it with pride at the same time. Her courage was on the level of survivors of concentration camps, where inmates who lived through the horror told how they concentrated on thinking about beauty, art and food to pull through. So it was with the cellar children and their mother. The stoicism and strength of them all was simply towering; set against the simple cruelty exerted by Fritzl, it dwarfed him and his diabolical scheme.

It appears that Elisabeth did teach her children about God, the Catholic faith she had learned at home and about trips with her mother and siblings. Her father had not been a churchgoer, but he expected his family to keep up public appearances and to attend Mass regularly. The faith was passed on in the cellar dungeon – when the family was eventually freed, teenager Stefan and 5-year-old Felix wondered if the moon was God. To them it seemed a splendid and wonderful thing, the personification in heaven of the being their mother had told them watched over them all. The damage done to these children who lived in the cellar all their young lives will take years to assess. The CO_2 output increased with the arrival of each child. With the birth of Felix in 2002 it quadrupled. For hours at a time the inmates of the cellar were reduced to lolling around on their beds like divers with the bends, their systems struggling to cope with the air starvation. This torpor was how they spent much of the last years underground.

When Natascha Kampusch was freed from her cellar dungeon after eight years, during which time she had been threatened with gas, explosives and the constant fear that her captor might just not return one day, she claimed that these threats had paled when compared with the agony of toothache caused by the lack of sunlight, vitamins and a regular trip to the dentist. Like her, all the Amstetten cellar family had chronic tooth decay, and dealing with her children's agony armed only with aspirin was a major challenge for Elisabeth, who herself had lost most of her teeth by the time she was freed. The agony of toothache is just one of the memories that will always be with them; they escaped from the cellar but will never be able to escape their experiences in it.

Unlocking the children's true feelings towards Fritzl will be a monumental task in itself. What do they think of him? He brought them presents, kissed them, stroked their hair, ate Christmas dinners with them and showed them pictures from the world beyond the cellar. It was Alice without the Wonderland. He bought them Christmas presents wrapped in gaily coloured paper, perfume and dresses for Elisabeth who had no one to show them off to but him. But he also beat them, kept them prisoner and stood them before him, saying 'Don't even think about trying to get beyond that door because it's electrified, and if you do, you will all certainly die.' Police later found this claim was a cruel bluff, but it added an extra dimension of terror for the loving mother who had long ago given up caring about her own fate, and who now lived for her children alone.

What did they think when they saw him take their mother into the rubber-lined recess where she slept? Sometimes he stayed overnight, his satisfied snoring reverberating around the walls, a terrible vision of perverted love. What did their still-forming minds think when he came to sit with them to eat pizza and he told them of what had been happening in his world – a world their mother had told them was false and not for them?

And yet Elisabeth, this most incredible of women, held it all together as each day a little more of her died inside that tomb. It is no wonder that Dr Albert Reiter, who would eventually become her saviour, says of her: 'It's no exaggeration when I say she is the strongest woman I have ever met. I don't think it is beyond the bounds of reason to say she has superhuman powers.'

6. Deception as Art

'She's gone.' With two syllables, Josef Fritzl told his family that Elisabeth – the runaway, the problem child, the rebel – had decided to flee the nest. His delivery was low-key, exasperated, the sagging shoulders and the raised brow portraying a father who had done his best but could do no more. The charade continued for 24 hours. Then the next 24 years.

He told the widow Danielczyk, who lived near by, and his friend Paul Hoera. Years later, the baker Gunther Pramreiter whose premises were next door to the Ybbsstrasse residence recalls: 'They told me he looked so believable. He'd been downcast, "Liesl, she's gone." If he wasn't upset he certainly looked it, they all agreed.'

But Paul Hoera – who, like the others, later recalled how the groundwork had already been prepared – says: 'Everyone around here knew she'd caused him a lot of trouble. Looking back, I suppose he did go out of his way to paint her as a wrong one in the year before she went. Do that enough times and when the event itself happens, you tend to swallow the version as offered, don't you?'

Pramreiter too admitted that perhaps he should have seen something. 'Fritzl bought the basics from me and we were on speaking terms, although you couldn't classify us as pals. But if anyone asked him about Elisabeth he'd make sure they knew the story. There was only one other time that he stopped and spoke to me at length about anything else, and that was in 1998, when the schoolgirl Natascha Kampusch got snatched in Vienna. That case fascinated him. He spoke about it a lot.'

The Fritzl clan were lined up like obedient little soldiers. Rosemarie dabbed at the tears which fell freely down her face. She never thought she would lose a child like this, but the proof seemed to be incontrovertible.

'Your sister is gone and I don't expect she'll be back,' said Fritzl, scanning the eyes of his remaining children for any flashes of disbelief or truculence. 'Work hard and don't disappoint your mother – and you'll not turn out like her.' She was immediately cast as the bad apple that no one could save.

It was left to Rosemarie to file the missing person's report with Amstetten police after Elisabeth had spent her first lonely and fear-filled night in the dungeon. Dressed in her best clothes, she went to the front desk to give the duty officer the bare facts of the case. But as soon as she came to give Elisabeth's age, the eyes of the police officer glazed over. Missing children are one thing, but the law classified 18-year-old Elisabeth as a woman. An adult. And one who had made dry runs in getting away from her obviously unhappy home in the past. The forms were duly filled in and Rosemarie handed over a photograph of her daughter, but it had the flavour of an exercise in futility even then. It was clear that she would not rank highly on the list of priorities for the nation's law en-forcers. Which is exactly what Fritzl the planner knew: kidnap and incarcerate Elisabeth on the wrong side of her majority and he risked the police actually taking her disappearance seriously. Hide her away as an adult and hers was no tragedy but a simple statistic. He had to hand it to himself – he'd thought of everything.

One month later, Josef Fritzl had taken care of his covert house dweller like clockwork. He entered the dungeon daily, hardened himself to her pleas for freedom, kept the fridge-freezer stocked with food and reinforced his instruction to tenants that no one was to enter his cellar area 'on pain of eviction'. On one of these nocturnal trysts with his daughter he produced pen and paper and instructed her to write what would be one of several notes over the coming years. He ensured that, in the house above, letters and school essays of Liesl were at hand. They would prove the veracity of the masquerade he was about to carry out.

> *Dear Papa and Mama,*
>
> *I have decided to move away to be independent. I am with people who care about me and I am safe. Please do not worry about me or come and look for me. This is my decision, my life. Please give my love to the family.*
>
> *S. X*

Whether or not Fritzl had to beat the forgery out of his daughter is not known. Her spirit was not entirely broken in those early days and weeks. But he obtained the letter and, climbing into his trusty E-class Mercedes, he drove to the hometown of his hero, Adolf Hitler, and posted the letter back to the family address in Ybbsstrasse.

Armed with it, and the specimens of his daughter's handwriting, he then took himself off to the local police station where he spun the yarn about her having talked about joining some strange sect in the months before she vanished. The handwriting on the letter matched that of her essays, the postmark of Braunau am Inn seemingly proof that she was off and under her own steam; she was now an adult in an adult world.

Elisabeth's fate was sealed. The police investigation, such as it was, was parked in the pending tray where it would remain for almost a quarter of a century.

Fritzl reinforced his tale, like he reinforced his cellar, with patience and care. The neighbour Danielczyk recalls: 'For weeks, months afterwards, he would go off in his car and not come back for hours on end. When I saw him he would say: "This time I tried Linz." Or Graz, or Vienna. He said he was out trawling the streets, looking for Elisabeth. "I know it's probably hopeless, but her mother worries so. I couldn't live with myself if I didn't do my best for her." Her story was in the local rag and he was quoted saying how cut up he was at losing his daughter. He said he went to places like the West Bahnhof in Vienna, where the druggies and prostitutes hung out, and went to some squatters' place in Linz. He really looked like the concerned dad, running around trying to do his best for his little girl.'

In actuality, he was using the fake expeditions to buy supplies for the concrete hiding place. He ferreted out the materials he needed, like a spy on a mission, gauging always the distance from the Ybbsstrasse home and whether or not it was likely any locals would be inside.

While he shopped at a small cluster of supermarkets and discount stores, most of his purchases were at a store called Metro in Linz. A wholesale outlet for small businesses and restaurants, Fritzl wrangled himself a card to shop there cheaply; he could buy frozen pizzas by the dozen, frozen vegetables in giant sacks, catering bags of pasta.

Cheapness ran through Fritzl like the lettering in a stick of rock. Along with cold, calculating evil, it was one of his defining characteristics. But on one of his mystery shopping expeditions, as he placed his goods on the moving band at the check-out, he was horrified to hear a voice behind him.

'Hey, Sepp. What're you buying here then?'

It was a neighbour, and one of the items in Fritzl's shopping trolley was, along with the comestibles, nappies. He turned, the gears of his quick-thinking brain crashing into place, cranking to find a quick, plausible retort. He was lucky that the voice was paying little attention to the goods as they were scanned by the girl at the till.

Pointing to the cashier, Fritzl said, 'I've managed to blag myself a card for this place by sleeping with the staff.'

His friend looked away from the nappies and towards the cashier. They both laughed, the question on his neighbour's lips forgotten as Fritzl whisked the nappies away into a bag and out of sight. The friend forgot the incident until years later, when he read that Metro had been Fritzl's main source of supplies for his cellar family. He was safe this time, but he would have to be more careful.

As Elisabeth festered and deteriorated in her artificially lit chamber, the weeks turned to months and the months to years. The story of the cult, and its Svengali-like grip on her, became accepted fact. To Rosemarie and her siblings she was a child frozen in time, the last pictures of her on the mantelpiece the only evidence that she had ever existed. In time, Rosemarie cleared out her room, gave her clothes to charity shops, bundled up her favourite toys from childhood into boxes and stuffed them in a storeroom. The psychological impact of losing her daughter was masked by Rosemarie as she took on more chores, working longer and longer hours. During the years before the cellar became a reality Fritzl had moved to isolate his wife from his daily life. He still needed his wife's efforts at the guest house to finance his dabbling in real estate. Now that his master plan was up and running, they became ever more distant with one another.

By the time Kerstin was born in 1989 the lie had been told long enough and often enough to be believed by everyone in Amstetten. Elisabeth's friends, her acquaintances – the neighbours she knew to say hello to as well as the complete strangers – no one doubted her father's story about the cult. The years passed, unknown to her, as her tormentor continued his journey of sexual fulfilment and intrigue.

The arrival of Stefan a year later prompted Fritzl to think that he might need to expand the cavern; the birth of baby Lisa on 29 August, 1992, acted as the catalyst for it. The cover would be the construction of a swimming pool in the grounds of the house, something that would mask the mountains of earth that would need to be shifted from the warren that existed on no official plans. Police estimate he removed some 190 tons of earth and bricks in sacks – no mean feat for a man of pensionable age, and proof of the strength that Elisabeth knew she could never fight against. He had to lug the detritus in sacks through the small opening of the secret cellar to dispose of in skips above ground. This was the perfect cover for the enlargement of the cellar complex.

But first he had to get rid of Rosemarie and make space for himself, and to do so he arranged for her to take over control of a second guest house, this time much nearer Amstetten, and sent her off there to manage the place. But even without his wife on hand to see what he was doing, this was perhaps the riskiest period for Fritzl during all the long years of subterfuge. He enlisted the help of his son Josef to assist him in digging out the swimming pool. But when Josef wasn't around, he would be barrowing earth out by the ton from the cellar, aided below ground by his captive daughter.

Residents of his house as well as neighbours recall the constant churning of a cement mixer, the arrival and departure of empty, later fully laden, skips. All the while, underground and unseen, Elisabeth Fritzl was literally clawing at dirt with her bare hands to carve out more space for herself and her children. The extra space was created by a passageway to a pre-existing basement area under the old part of the property which nobody knew of, apart from Fritzl. The concealed cellar was soundproofed and consisted of a corridor 5 metres long, a storage area and three small open cells, all connected by narrow passageways, a basic cooking area and bathroom facilities, followed by two sleeping areas, which were equipped with two beds each. It covered an area of approximately 55 square metres. The ceilings were 1.7 metres at their highest.

When the cellar extension was complete the next diabolical phase of the master plan kicked in: moving out Lisa to become part of the world of light. The child was sickly, prone to coughing fits and violent shivering. She was also extremely noisy – a 'screamer', in Fritzl's words – a child who, he feared, might actually, one day, be heard through the metres of earth, iron and concrete which covered the bunker, and who disturbed the quiet of his dungeon refuge. After informing Elisabeth that he was taking the child upstairs to live, he made her write another letter, forcing her to bury herself still further in his lies. Her letter would perpetuate the fiction that she had abandoned the child because she could no longer bring her up.

'Dear parents,' she penned in her distinctive rolling script. 'I pass on my little daughter Lisa to you. Look after her carefully.' It was on 19 May, 1993, that Fritzl got up from the kitchen table in his upstairs flat after hearing the doorbell ring. He affected surprise when he collected a cardboard box on the doorstep with Lisa, now nine months old, inside. Of course there was no genuine surprise; he had put the box there and rigged the doorbell to ring on a timer.

This single act, for Amstetten chief executive Dr Lenze, stands out as a sign of the complexity of the Fritzl plot. 'The house was in multiple occupation, people came and went at all times, he couldn't control that, yet he needed to dump the baby, and then be the one to answer the door and get the package. Think about it – he rigged up a doorbell to ring, probably with another of his remote controls, just seconds after he walked into the room. He would have told his wife, "Don't worry, I'll get it," gone downstairs and been the one to find the baby. There was almost no chance that in that one minute anyone else would see the baby. And even if they had, he would've been there seconds later to take control. It shows the incredible lengths he went to to hide this from the world.'

In the letter he showed his incredulous wife, she read, 'You are probably wondering why you are hearing from me only now, also since this letter comes along with a human surprise.' Elisabeth added, in the note dictated by her rapist father, 'I have been breastfeeding her for six and a half months. Now she only drinks milk out of a bottle, everything else she eats off a spoon.' Elisabeth wrote that she found herself 'incapable' of caring for her daughter and hoped she wouldn't be too much trouble to her parents. A psychiatrist who would examine the letter many years later said that it was phrased as if Elisabeth was simply requesting some respect and tolerance for her alternative lifestyle.

To say Rosemarie Fritzl was taken aback was an understatement. She spent long minutes just looking at the child, reciting 'oh my goodness' over and over, as if the mantra might deliver up some answers. Her domestic martinet of a husband had already concluded that they had no choice; their daughter Elisabeth was no good but she had done the right thing in surrendering to them a child she could not look after.

'We will do what is right,' he told Rosemarie, before they got dressed to go, first, to the police station, and secondly, to the youth authorities in the town centre.

The authorities were bureaucratic mirror images of the Ybbsstrasse neighbours and residents. They saw nothing beyond what they wanted to see. The charade said respectable family man, good solid citizen, with a strong marriage, a churchgoing wife and money in the bank. Of course, they might have dug a little deeper and discovered a rape conviction, arson enquiries, links to other unsolved sex crimes that would emerge only years later, and a daughter who ran away from his household when she was a teenager. They might have done these things. But they didn't. The shrewd and wily Fritzl knew the mindset of the authorities, just as he knew the mindset of the Ybbsstrasse community. They would be no bother, he thought, and he was right.

'Mr and Mrs Fritzl have recovered from their first shock,' the youth officer in Amstetten wrote in a report made five days after Lisa had been 'found'. A worthy lady with a clipboard had been to see the family and had drunk coffee from a small Meissen service Rosemarie owned. The lady was impressed and added in her report: 'The Fritzl family lovingly takes care of Lisa and would like to keep on doing so. We think it is in the best interests of the child to be brought up by the grandparents who are obviously responsible and caring guardians.' One year later the couple adopted Lisa – but the baby train was still rolling.

On 15 December, 1994, shortly after midnight, the next child, Monika, was found. She was nine months old. This time the child wasn't placed in a cardboard box but in a children's pushchair in the hallway. A couple of minutes later the phone rang and Rosemarie Fritzl answered it.

When she seemed to hear her daughter's voice on the other end, Elisabeth told her to take care of her child. 'I've just left her in front of your house.'

The phone call was curious for two reasons. The first, because it was her own flesh and blood, her daughter who had run away from her home but not her heart. The second, because Josef had just had the phone number changed. He was, it seems, fed up getting calls from irate tenants, or from creditors, or from people he simply didn't want to be bothered by.

'How did she get the number?' Rosemarie asked her husband when he came back from making the call to his wife from a phone box two streets away.

Fritzl almost bit his lip in frustration, cursed under his breath. It had been easy to go into the cellar and menace his captive into speaking into a recording machine. But he had not taken the factor of the new, unlisted number into account. Fortunately for Fritzl, Rosemarie's lack of education and low self-esteem meant she did not think to pursue the matter further. Make a note, he told himself; must be more careful.

A third child, Alexander, the survivor of Elisabeth's twin boys born in the gloom, was the last of this inexplicable tribe. Born on 28 April, 1996, he was 15 months old when he was brought out of the cellar. His birth would be followed in 2002 by the arrival of Elisabeth's youngest child, Felix, whose fate would not be as sunny as Alexander's. Felix was to spend the first five years of his life underground, condemned to a wretched and cramped existence, before being brought out of the cellar and into the light.

Twenty-one times the social workers came to the Fritzl
house. Twenty-one times they sat and sipped coffee and
munched on sugar-coated home-made biscuits, scratch-
ing notes on to forms, such as 'the Fritzls lovingly take
care of their children'; 'everything seems to be in order
in the Fritzl residence'; 'the children make good progress.
They are frequently seen with books and cassettes from
the public library and seem quick and keen learners. The
grandfather seems strict, perhaps sometimes over-strict,
but there is a good family structure and the children are
doing well at school.'

Susanne Parb, the woman who knew of her friend's
torment when she was a child, beats herself up that she
did nothing when the news spread around small-town
Amstetten that babies were being deposited by the long-
vanished Elisabeth on her father's doorstep. 'When the
babies started arriving I knew it wasn't right. Elisabeth
hated her father – she would never have left her own
children with him. I should've picked up on that,
should've reported it. I'm mad at myself that I didn't.'
But, sadly, Elisabeth and the others consigned to the
dungeon remained Fritzl's abiding, dark secret.

To maintain these parallel worlds took a mind of
incredible criminal agility, according to British clinical
psychologist Dr Kristina Downing-Orr. 'It was as if there
was no remorse, no empathy for his daughter, for his
grandchildren, for his wife. That's what's chilling.' She
thinks he imprisoned Elisabeth because he didn't want
the relationship to end at 18, when she would reach her
majority and be off. 'Perhaps she would go out and have
boyfriends of her own. Perhaps he was a bit afraid he'd

be caught, that she'd go out and tell people, and that led him to imprison her in this dungeon basement. It's that calculating sociopathic methodology, that kind of logic, that I find particularly chilling. But fortunately, it's very rare; we rarely see that kind of behaviour. Unfortunately, Elisabeth Fritzl and her dungeon children did.'

A matter of yards separated the families but it might as well have been continents. Rosemarie was exhausted at the end of each demanding day but she was an adoring grandmother. She shepherded the children to music lessons – Lisa learned the German flute, Monika and Alexander the trumpet – and ran them around to other extra-curricular school activities.

'Everybody admired her for being so strong,' the children's former music teacher remembers. Only once did Rosemarie speak to him about Elisabeth. 'She lost her voice and had tears in her eyes talking about her daughter, saying that she was a follower of some kind of sect and that she missed her daughter very much.'

Rosemarie went to church with the children on Sunday and encouraged them all to do extra homework, especially Alexander, who had spent 15 months in the cellar – six months longer than Lisa and Monika – before he joined the 'upstairs' children. Did he ever have flashbacks to a time and a place of such horror?

Fritzl never attended St Mary's Church in Amstetten with his family, or indeed any other church on a regular basis. Police theorize he probably used the time his wife and upstairs family were absent to sneak into the cellar for more abuse. The local Catholic priest Franz

Halbartschlager became a close friend as a result of the Fritzl family's regular visits to his church, when Elisabeth was in their prayers. He knew of the rumours that she had run away to join a sect. Years later, when he was called to give Kerstin the last rites, he immediately recognized the similarities between her and her three siblings who had not spent their lives in the cellar. 'The three children taken in by the Fritzl family received their first communion here. When I was asked to go to the hospital and I heard her name I was stunned. I was of course able to see similarities between Kerstin and the other children. But while they were healthy she had obviously suffered from her life underground. She was pale and her lips were swollen.' He adds: 'Fritzl led an incredible double life.'

Dubanovsky, one of the Ybbsstrasse tenants, recalls what locals dubbed 'the time of the storks', when children appeared with the regularity of a courier service. 'When I wanted to move out I asked Fritzl if there was some kind of period of notice before I could leave, but he said that he didn't care because I lived in one of the three flats he didn't want to rent out any more. He explained that he was going to keep them for the three grandchildren living with him, because they were getting older. That sounded like a logical explanation to me. I knew the kids quite well, I always had funny little conversations with them. I met them often because I was allowed to put my moped in their courtyard and Alexander was always saying that he wanted to have a motorbike too. His grandmother then said, "Yes, of course. Keep on dreaming."

'I'd say the relationship within the family was all right. Of course sometimes Fritzl lost his temper and started shouting at the kids. When he did, that was usually inside the flat, and I could hear him bellowing as my living space was just metres away from theirs.

'I holiday in Thailand regularly and so he started talking to me about it. He then let me know that he was always looking for women when he was there, and he knew where you could get sex for little money. Once I said to him that it was really easy to get all sorts of drugs there. He then said that he didn't want to have anything to do with that and that he was worried about it getting easier to get drugs for young people in Austria.

'Then he said, "That's why you've got to lock kids away these days." Spooky, eh? We started to talk more and more, and in the end we could speak about basically everything. He always told me about the house, the work he did on it and so on. Officially he was already retired by the time I moved in. He said that he'd been working abroad for a while on a power plant and he made good money there. At the end of the day, he was an old man. He and his wife started to have problems, getting out of breath as they walked up the stairs, that sort of thing.

'Of all of Fritzl's proper children, I mean the ones he had in his marriage, the only one I knew was Sepp. He was like Fritzl's servant. He must be about 37 or 38 – and still he did everything his father told him to. He was really oppressed by his father, who didn't want him to move out at all. He had his own flat in the house, and Fritzl always told him to stay at home, and that he'd take care of everything for him. I remember when I was 20, Fritzl ran a little inn close to his place, and Sepp was always there, getting shouted at.

'Fritzl went to the cellar every day, but that was none of my business. I thought that he might have a hobby that he was going down there for. Modelmaking or something. That seemed normal to me. He always went to bed at 10 o'clock, and before that he walked around the whole house once to check if everything was in order. Whenever I saw him at this time, he showed up at a different spot somewhere in the house.

'Rosemarie? Well, she was just a very quiet, mousy woman, one who you could see was definitely treated badly by her very authoritarian husband. I don't think that she was ever down into the cellar, at least I never saw her going down. She was very caring towards the children. In 1998, I bought myself a new home entertainment system and I turned up the volume a bit too much, so Fritzl came down and told me to be quiet. Some weeks later, Rosemarie came to me and wanted to buy my old TV. It was a nice colour TV, made by Grundig, and already had teletext on it. Rosemarie absolutely wanted to buy it, so I sold it to her for 1,500 schillings. I asked myself what they needed it for because I knew that they already had two TVs in their flat. Fritzl later said, "I'll give it to the children." Except it was children that no one knew about. They saw the world on my old TV and I didn't know a damn thing.'

It was during Elisabeth's fourteenth year in the cellar that Fritzl embarked on the second of his selfish odysseys to Thailand. When he first went in the 1970s with Paul Hoera there was no living creature dependent on him making it back safe and sound. Going for a four-week holiday, knowing that his daughter's life, and the lives of his children, depended on him making it back safe and sound, compounded his secret pleasure at her utter helplessness. Although he talked of a timer on the cellar door that would open 'if anything happened to me', electrical experts later found that the timer did not exist. Fritzl didn't care; he had pulled off his scheme and he celebrated with some good old-fashioned R&R in the fleshpots of Bangkok and beyond.

Hoera recalls: 'He seemed to have a spring in his step. I remember he had a very long massage from a young Thai girl at the beach. He really loved that. Once I saw how Josef bought an evening dress and racy lingerie for a very slim woman on the beach in Pattaya. He got really angry when he realized I'd seen him. Then he told me that he had "a girlfriend on the side". The items were meant for her. He told me not to tell his wife. I think we know now who they were for.'

Videos have surfaced of Fritzl enjoying himself on the beach, apparently without a care in the world. They are testament to his utter callousness towards his cellar family and also to his ability to compartmentalize them in his mind, just as he compartmentalized them in his house.

Roswitha Zmug, the owner of the Gasthof zur Post restaurant in Aschbach, just outside Amstetten, remembers his long-suffering wife and her adoration for her family, the wellspring of her sanity. 'She took the place on in 1993 just before the first child arrived, but had to give up when the second child arrived just over a year later. He never did any work – not that I could see anyway. He just came in from time to time to make sure she was working and have a quick drink, or something to eat, and then he left. It was always her and her children who did the work. They also had an apartment upstairs where she often stayed overnight with the children. He never stayed here. The business never went really well, mainly because the place was so run-down. He was too mean to invest any money in it and he didn't make much of an effort in helping her.

'Fritzl did lots of business that wasn't legal; at the very best it was borderline. I remember that he faked a load of bills to an air-conditioning system company. He took the letterhead off the invoice and wrote a second bill to make the price less. He then sent a cheque with the altered bill back to the air-conditioning firm. But they spotted the forged bill and there was a big legal battle . . . Then there was another time he ripped me off. I decided that I'd like to take over the business and had to deal with him during the negotiations. He wrote a contract which included a list of all the property that he added, such as the kitchen and so on, which I had to buy off him. I also had to compensate him for all the building work done. Later I spoke to the owner of the property that I was renting and she told me it was actually her stuff. It was a lot of money, over 100,000 schillings.

'I disliked him intensely even before that. He was always so nice on the surface to everyone, but really he was just superior and arrogant. I don't think he respected anybody. It was clear Rosemarie had no sort of relationship with him. She did all the work, and he just took advantage of that. I'm positive she knew nothing about what had happened to Elisabeth; she was just totally overworked and struggling to get by from one day to the next.'

On 2 March, 1998, an event occurred that was to spellbind Josef Fritzl; it was the disappearance of a 10-year-old girl on her way to school in Vienna. Fritzl could not possibly know what had happened to Natascha Kampusch – that she was to be held in a secret, soundproofed cellar much like the one he had carved out beneath his home – but he was fascinated by it. He would talk endlessly about it, not knowing that Wolfgang Priklopil, her abductor, was a man like himself with a penchant for the forbidden. Less than 200 kilometres separated the clandestine kingdoms of Priklopil and Fritzl but they were, somehow, inextricably bound together. When it was finally to be all over, the mistakes that the police had made in trapping Priklopil would be scrutinized anew to spot the wrong turnings in the road during the long years of Elisabeth's gruesome ordeal.

PART THREE
Miracle

7. The End is Nigh

The Villa Ostende in Linz is bathed in pink light and music pulsates through the walls. It is a hackneyed cliché of a brothel, with pink lights in a plastic tube that thread their way up the pink-carpeted stairs through the pink corridors to the pink bedrooms. The lounge where punters gather to choose a partner is the only one not to join in the colour scheme: it is brown and beige, with a 1970s-style Naugahyde sofa beneath three 'artworks' – a headless nude, a lithograph of an Apache warrior and what appears to be a Made-in-Taiwan replica of his shield next to it. Overall, it is a sad place where enforced jollity is the order of the day. It caters to the men who have no partner, or those who want to spice their life up, the stag-night crowd who insist on 'one last fling' for the bridegroom-to-be, and cheating sales reps spending their meal allowances on sex.

It also catered to Josef Fritzl. As sex with Rosemarie had long ago ceased and his libido showed no signs of slowing down, the Villa Ostende was one of a number of outlets where he satisfied his urges. Elisabeth was suffering in the cellar but, in the world above her, revolutions had taken place in social mores and sex drugs. Prostitution is legal in Austria and regulated by the state. Prostitutes are considered to be self-employed, and since 1986 they have been required to pay taxes. They are entitled to welfare and other social security payments.

A social research group carried out a study in the
1960s which declared that half of all Austrian males visit
a prostitute at least once in their lifetimes. There is a
sexually tolerant air abroad towards brothels and working
girls that sometimes seems out of step with the naturally
conservative and straight-laced atmosphere that exists in
the rest of Austrian society. Clubs like Villa Ostende had
their own website and advertised in local papers; local
businesses held raunchy lads-only parties there. Elisabeth's father, never satisfied by venting his desire upon
her alone, was a subscriber to online pharmacies where
he purchased prolific amounts of Viagra and other sex
drugs for his special nights out at Villa Ostende. He
would prime himself on a cocktail of drugs and energy
drinks such as Red Bull, telling friends, 'This will allow
you to go at it for hours.' But the pleasure was secondary.

Sexual violence is found in almost every country and
research indicates it crosses all class boundaries. Fritzl
enjoyed inflicting abuse from the days when he first found
the opposite sex attractive. He has an exaggerated sense
of masculinity, a preference for impersonal sexual relationships as opposed to emotional bonding, and views having
many sexual partners as a badge of honour. Fritzl never
saw women as partners to be respected and honoured; he
saw them as opponents to be conquered and quashed.
There is, perhaps, irony in the choice of room that Fritzl
favoured above all others in the Villa Ostende. On his
nights there, in his handmade suits and awash with
cologne, his hairpiece firmly affixed and his shoes brightly
polished, he merely swapped one dungeon for another.

In the club's basement, to cater for the clientele whose tastes tended more towards the exotic, is a filthy cell, complete with bars and iron door. Known as 'The Sex Vault' to its regulars, the dungeon was the setting for the fetishists to get their kicks. For Fritzl, it was home from home.

One sex worker, who was one of his favourites before she could no longer stomach his perverted demands, revealed how he pleasured himself by tying her to a makeshift cross complete with dangling manacles. 'Call me teacher,' he demanded, punching her kidneys, slapping her across the face and buttocks. 'You *will* show me respect, bitch!'

'He stared at me with those ice-cold eyes,' says the woman, now in her thirties. In a good light and with make-up, she could be said to resemble his daughter Elisabeth. She called herself Lola, came from Graz when she was a child, and drifted into prostitution to support herself and her only daughter. 'I was hired by him many times and he was sick beyond imagination. He chose me because he said he liked young, plump – but not fat – girls who were happy to submit to him. He always had to be called "teacher" and I wasn't allowed to enter into conversation with him unless he initiated it. If I was required to speak, I had to preface the start of every phrase with "master" and finish it with "master, my master". He insisted that I wore black high heels and only tan-coloured nylon stockings, never any other colour. I also had to wear bright-red lipstick to "look the proper slut" in his words, and he always insisted I kept my knickers on during sex; he'd simply pull them to one side.

He breathed heavily all the while, his eyes were bulbous. He was terrifying. But hey, I needed the money – we all do. And while it was 150 euros for vanilla sex, we could squeeze double that out of him for the extras.

'He'd pay to have sex inside the brothel dungeon, which I hated. It was dark and sinister and damp but his favourite place. He'd usually take me from behind, slap me about, call me names like "whore" and "bitch", satisfy himself and leave without another word. To think he was keeping his daughter and her children in a similar place a few kilometres away and abusing them sickens me now. I didn't even know his name.' Ironically, she came to identify him with the same name Elisabeth's friends had used decades earlier. 'Me and the girls just used to refer to him as "Dracula" because he often dressed in black and he looked, well, evil. I once asked him about his family and he told me, "I have none." I thought he was a lonely man – now I know he's a beast. He belongs in hell.'

Fritzl was a frequenter of the Villa Ostende and clubs like it for years. He started frequenting bordellos in the 1970s on the odd night out, before making it a regular weekly excursion. His appetite for violent sex increased in the 80s and 90s, according to the owner, Peter Stolz; a tempo fuelled by the sex potions he bought online. It was as the new millennium approached that his penchant for inflicting pain marked him out to the prostitutes as a customer to avoid.

Barman Christoph Flugel winces visibly at the memory of Fritzl. He worked at the Villa Ostende for six years, saw much of life, and much he would like to forget. Fritzl, however, he cannot. 'He loved inflicting pain and wanted some girls to act like a corpse. He was violent and into domination. Two of the girls actually said, "Never again with that guy." That's rare in this business. Ninety-five per cent of the guests are entirely normal, three per cent are slightly "derailed". Fritzl belonged to the last two per cent of extreme perverts. Fritzl would come regularly. As well as his bizarre sexual tastes, I'll never forget his stinginess. If he consumed drinks for €97 and paid with a €100 bill, he'd demand the €3 back.

'At the bar he was domineering. He acted the big shot with all the staff, always liked telling them what to do, how to do it. If he liked a girl he'd order champagne for her, but after a short while he'd start behaving like a headmaster with pupils and say things like, "Sit up straight!" or, "Don't talk nonsense!" Such behaviour is unusual in sex clubs.'

Villa Ostende is reputedly Austria's oldest bordello and Josef Fritzl, given his weakness for the Nazis and their way of doing things, would doubtless have been an admirer of the jackbooted SS officers and security police-men of the Third Reich who frequented it during the war years. Local newspapers even printed that Hitler himself had been a visitor, but this is doubtful.

Peter Stolz has described in even more graphic detail the things that Fritzl liked to do. 'He was a strange, stingy character. He liked trips to the dungeon with young girls he selected personally. He'd play an aggressive rapist hunting down his victim. He insisted that the rape had to be "real". He came here up to three times a week around the time he put his daughter in the cellar.

'Everything revolved around subjugation and humiliation: their pain, his pleasure. He liked, for instance, to put girls in a sack and then tighten it so hard that his victim had difficulty breathing inside. He'd tell her, "I want to hear you gasping for breath, I want to see you on the point of dying, but I will let you out again."

'He wanted to push girls to the brink of death so that he was in a position where he could decide whether they lived or died. He wanted, in effect, to play God. He had a God complex that was out of control. He was extremely perverse and clearly needed to torture in order to be sexually satisfied. Fritzl also got his kicks from acting out rape fantasies with hookers he insisted were heavily made up to "look like sluts" in scarlet lipstick. He'd be the predatory sex attacker and they'd be his terrified, screaming victims. Fritzl liked to beat the girls and, occasionally but not always, got a thrill from being battered by them. Most of the time, he wanted to be violent and aggressive and wanted to beat the girls or lash them with a whip.

'He visited two to three times a week and was one of my best customers as well as one of my worst. He always wanted all the works, but wanted to pay the least amount of money. And he had the most warped and perverted fantasies of anyone.' Stolz, the caring employer, does not ever say if he intervened to stop Fritzl from hurting the workforce.

Some 30 kilometres away is another Fritzl favourite called the Caribik Club. It is a riot of faux palm-fringed beach huts and rum cocktails, sand imported from a local quarry and drinks with umbrellas in them. The Caribik is another sex temple, this one devoted to swingers who are invited to loosen up with rum cocktails before romping on the rattan furniture that lies scattered around beneath paper palm fronds. Whatever Fritzl's wife Rosemarie may have been – naive, stupid, battered, abused or simply stoic – she could never be classed as a swinger. Yet she accompanied him there, not to indulge herself, but to fulfil his need to humiliate her, to exercise once again that overarching need for power.

Paul Stocker, a local builder who met Fritzl when he was trying to sell his home in 1997, agreed to go with him to the club 'for a boys' night out' in 1997. 'Fritzl told me that someone of our age can have a lot of fun with sex. He said you needed to take three tablets – Viagra, Levitra and Cialis. He said: "The pills kick in one after the other and you can go for it like a bull."

'A week later I was in the Caribik by myself when I saw an elderly couple come in. They looked just like an old pair that you might see sitting on a bench in a park feeding the pigeons. I was speechless when I realized who it was. It was Fritzl with his wife. He obviously knew his way around there. She went without a word to stand in the corner and he immediately started working on another visitor, who was obviously not having a good time with the person she was with at that point. As they heated up together, he forced Rosemarie to watch, kept on glancing over at her squirming. His pleasure, his kicks, came solely from making his wife uncomfortable. It was a sickening spectacle.'

Fritzl's relentless quest for hedonistic pleasure ran in parallel with his duties in keeping the secret cave clan alive. Age and weariness were beginning to tell on him. He found he couldn't move about so easily and suffered chest pains if he tried to shift heavy objects.

He kept to his routine of telling the family he would be 'in the cellar' at around 9 a.m. two to three mornings each week when he would check on his brood, see what they wanted or needed. Sometimes he came armed with clothing catalogues which he allowed Elisabeth to peruse if he felt she needed a new dress. The choice was rarely made by her; the control remained firmly with him.

Fritzl began toying with the notion of perhaps finding a solution to their continued existence; he knew in his heart of hearts that they would have to be released one day or die, because he wasn't getting any younger and, while timers controlled the mechanisms to keep them locked up, they could not be fed by remote control. He had created the underworld; now he toyed with various scenarios in his fevered mind about how to bring his underground family into the world of light but still keep his secret safe.

He knew the health of all the cellar inhabitants was suffering; Kerstin was fitting more and more while the boys were weak from lack of vitamins. Under pressure from Elisabeth in her last year in the cellar he brought in vitamin D supplements and an ultra-violet lamp as an ersatz sun for them to use. And as much (or as little) as he says he was concerned about the continuing incarceration, he was also aware that the strange routine he had followed for over two decades had not gone totally unnoticed by neighbours. There were the shopping trips at odd hours to buy the comestibles, the cleaning agents, the clothes. Curtains twitched when he lugged great boxes and sacks, in and out, in and out, from the entrance to this clandestine world.

'I have to say, like everyone else, in retrospect, that I found it odd he needed a wheelbarrow to trundle supplies into the basement area,' says Walter Wemer, who lived next door to Fritzl for 11 years. 'What's he doing down there? I thought. But I never thought reality could be as bad as it was eventually proved to be.'

There has been much speculation that Fritzl's son Josef, or 'Sepp', who continued to live in the house, was somehow implicated in his father's dastardly project. A former neighbour in an interview for this book said he routinely took on caretaker responsibilities for his father, which included going into the cellar area. Sabine Kirschbichler recalls: 'Whenever we needed something, for example if a tile in the flat was broken or there was something wrong with the electricity, Josef junior used to go into the cellar and get replacement parts or tools to fix it. I noticed that he always locked the door immediately after he came out. It was also unusual in a rented house like this that tenants weren't allowed to use the cellar to store things, which is normal when you rent a small flat in Austria.' Of course Frau Kirschbichler, like everyone else, never saw the complexity of the warren that Josef senior had constructed.

Despite the speculation of neighbours and friends, the police have not classified Fritzl's son as a suspect; they are treating the crimes of the father as being a solo effort from beginning to end. It seems that Josef junior was duped by his father as thoroughly as were the rest of his family.

One thing that shows how he was planning to call time on his double life in the dungeon was the fact that he helped Elisabeth to order presents using her own name and have them delivered to Ybbsstrasse. A search of a confidential credit rating database shows that one 'Elisabeth Fritzl' born on 8 April, 1966, had arranged for items to be sent to her Ybbsstrasse address for Xmas 2007. Police believe these were an attempt by Fritzl to help Elisabeth to win back the trust of her family and test their reaction to the fact that she was emerging back into the real world. At the time of writing, the police continue to trawl the three databases of all credit card holders in Austria to see what else she purchased.

It was a high-stress and high-risk business. Had the police been following up the missing person case – and bearing in mind the fact that Elisabeth was a wanted person in her own right for child abandonment – then sending gifts in her name and giving her address as Ybbsstrasse 40 was a dangerous move and one that could have rung all sorts of alarm bells. It shows the lengths to which Fritzl was prepared to go in order to call time on his parallel universe. This life-on-the-edge drama had once given him surges of sexual excitement but, with his heart under increasing strain, it was one more hassle he could do without.

There is also the theory that Fritzl may even have been considering building another, larger underground cellar further away from Ybbsstrasse. Just a few streets away in Waidhofnerstrasse is a small house situated on a large plot. The garden is better screened from neighbours at the rear than the Ybbsstrasse address, and at the front there is a small, light-yellow property with wooden windows.

Otto Popp, a neighbour, says Fritzl told him he wanted to develop the plot. 'What I found really strange was that two years ago, he turned up with a huge digger, and dug a huge number of holes. He was with his son. I remember him shouting a lot, and then overnight he carried on working and filled them all in. From what I could hear it sounded the soil wasn't right for whatever he was planning – but I never found out what that was as he didn't have any planning permission registered at that time. I told the police and they're planning on digging the garden up to see what he was doing there. But at the moment it's all a mystery.' For the moment, only Josef Fritzl knows the answer to whether he was considering a second cellar – a larger complex – at the new address.

Popp continues: 'Fritzl avoided contact during the building negotiations and was a very strange person. After buying the property he didn't even introduce himself to the neighbours. You only needed to look at the way he bossed the family around. The children were never loud, always quiet and walking behind the grandmother. He'd take them there and make them wait or help out as he did work on the house or garden.'

But while the life of the family above ground may not have been ideal, that of the family below was incomparably worse. Never in modern European history has a family been subjected to such prolonged sensory deprivation. Yet it was not their welfare that concerned Fritzl so much as a solution to what he saw as *his* problem – the problem of explaining them away should he choose to make the ultimate, final step that would end his Stygian world. A police source, speaking in 2008 on condition of anonymity, explained that Fritzl had been cooperating in interviews after the release of the cellar family. 'He says that in 2007 he first began to have the serious notion about bringing closure to the whole thing. The problem for him was how to do it, and this plagued him right until the end when events overtook whatever he was dreaming up. Essentially, he dreamed of having the clan re-emerge from the non-existent cult with them relating a story about wanting to have escaped sooner, but being unable to do so because of "pressures".

'He planned to say this cult was in another country, the Grail cult from the Czech Republic most likely, because he believed Austria was too small and the police would be able to pin down the lie. He felt confident he could bully the children into never revealing the secret of their horrific birth, life and experiences underground – but Elisabeth continued to worry him, and rightly so. Whatever arrangements they'd come to in the gloom, there was always the fear that his kidnapping, detention and rape of her would come out if she were free. Because he's essentially a creature of illimitable self-interest, it's become clear that at no time did the welfare of the clan take precedence in his mental juggling about what to do; as always it was all about him and how he hoped he could continue to hoodwink society that he was a proud, correct and upstanding fellow. He wanted it to play out, ulti-mately, that he was the "loving father" who somehow engineered the rescue of his daughter and her children.'

If they looked pale and ill – as they did – it was

the years of undernourishment and imprisonment at the hands of the mindbenders in the cult Elisabeth had taken up with. If Elisabeth was to be charged with child neglect, he would stand by her. His life was one massive subterfuge and he saw no reason to change that.

Fritzl has given away another element in his scheme to police interrogators; he was simply no longer finding Elisabeth attractive. Elisabeth had given him exactly the same number of children as his wife Rosemarie. Now he had lost interest in her, but he did not care for the wounds he had inflicted on her. Nothing. Josef Fritzl was incapable of that – the mark of the true psychopath.

Police note that, in the latter half of 2007 and 2008, Fritzl began dropping more and more hints to friends and neighbours about 'the sect' and the fact that he 'might be on to them'. There were, as usual, no details; just bogeymen off there somewhere beyond the horizon. As one police officer on the case puts it: 'In his half-baked plan it was supposed to appear as though the "bad mother" had finally come home with her three children.' Bad mother, hero dad, poor kids. A drama scripted by Josef Fritzl, Academy Award winner in duplicity and cunning.

Paul Hoera, the man who knew Fritzl as a 'good guy', who accompanied him on holiday, who shared what he thought were his innermost secrets when in reality he didn't even come close, recalls the evolution of a new Fritzl, a more questioning and uncertain Fritzl, in those last months before the earthquake hit Amstetten. The facts, learned through the filter of the media, set him thinking, like all the others touched by this strange, complex and deeply disturbing saga, that Fritzl the pal had been playing him like he played everyone else. 'Now I see that he was testing me out as a sounding board for the various scenarios that he was obviously playing out in his head. I suppose he was waiting to see how I'd react, log it, and then move on to another possibility. He was a crafty bastard.

'Back when the sprogs were arriving on his doorstep one by one he'd always call me and tell me about the letter from Elisabeth with it. I suppose I was his "benchmark of gullibility", if you will. It was like, if it passed the test with me, he'd go on to spread the fiction elsewhere. Trouble is, I was as stupid as every other Austrian, just swallowed it all, all down the years. I thought the Austrian police must be incredibly dumb not to have found a runaway girl in a country the size of a postage stamp, but Fritzl relied on that incredulity, didn't he? He relied on the image of things, not their reality; that was the central plank of everything he did.

'In the last – I don't know, I suppose – nine months before the whole jig was up, he was never off the phone, talking to me about everything from his health problems – he thought he had a dodgy heart – to his savings and investments, debts and mortgages. "I want to simplify my life, Paul," he said. "Reduce the stress." Christ! What stress had he coped with for the last quarter century?

'He also talked about "going away", mentioned the far east, although who knows if that wasn't just a smoke-screen while he thought about something else? He was, I believe, genuinely worried about his health in the last year before he got pinched. He had taken up swimming and was spending lots of money on various pills and herbal remedies. I think he finally realized that even someone with as much energy as he had has to come to an end sometime, and it really shook him. He liked a beer but he never drank that much, rarely smoked and certainly didn't do drugs – well, not mind-altering ones anyway. I read afterwards that he sucked down sex pills like they were sweets, but I guess they don't count.

'I remember one particular conversation I had with him in the last months before it all blew up. He said that he wished he could "go to his grave" being reunited with his daughter Elisabeth. And he asked me my opinion. "Do you think I should forgive her for what she's put me and Rosemarie through? I'm certain she's shaved years off the lives of both of us. I know she was unhappy at home, but we only ever had her best interests at heart." I think I said something to him like she'd be grown up now and would view her dad in a completely different way. I suspect the conversation illustrated, at some unfathomable level, his need to justify to himself what had taken place. A complex guy. I know now I only scratched the surface.'

Another man who scratched the surface, but wishes he had dug deeper, was Anton Kraushofer, now 68. He lives in a pretty, detached house with red geraniums in the flowerboxes and a view of snow-capped mountains in the distance. A river runs across the bottom of his garden; he has a dog at his feet and a glass of cool beer in his hand at lunchtimes. Kraushofer is enjoying his retirement and could never grasp why Fritzl seemed unable ever to let go and kick back from his frenetic activities.

'Yes, I knew Fritzl,' he recalls. 'It was sometime in 2004. I sold him a property in St Poelten that had six flats in all, with room for business space as well. He got in touch with me via the estate agent. I had nothing to do with him early on in the deal, just when it came to clinching it. It was Linzer Strasse 30 he was interested in and he turned up to sign on the dotted line and agree the money. He seemed an absolutely serious, very correct older man. He made a good impression on me, seemed a guy of solid values, one you wouldn't mind doing business with. He used the correct, formal way of greeting that people of my generation expect but which is sadly being eroded among the younger generation. He was also very well informed about the business of real estate, the extra costs that have to be incurred such as service charges on the apartments, that sort of thing. I didn't feel I was dealing with a dimwit or a time-waster.

'Everything was business in the half-dozen or so repeat meetings we had in which we talked about costs, the heating system, the electrics, that sort of thing. Only one time did we touch on anything personal and, now I know the whole story, I'm certain of one thing: he was buying this house for his family, both the upstairs ones as well as the cellar ones.

'I remember saying to him: "Herr Fritzl, I'm five years younger than you and I'm fed up with working. Chasing after rents and dealing with tenants who try to stiff you at every turn. I managed to save enough to build myself a house, and you already obviously have enough money to see you into your retirement, so why are you doing this? I mean, it's going to be years of work – you'll need

to do improvements to the property, see them through
and sort out new tenants, renovate the business properties. Why is a man of your age thinking about this?"

'He told me straight up: "I want it for my grandchildren. I have lots of them and don't really have the
space for them all." He came to me via an agent because
he thought the place was "a good prospect". I inherited
it from my grandparents. It had belonged to them for 40
or 50 years – I lived there myself. The flats are between
60 and 150 square metres each. I've never been inside his
other property on the Ybbsstrasse so I don't know how
he organized the inside or whether there was enough
space for his family. Presumably not, as he said he needed
more space.

'He transferred the money in a lump sum, cash to the
lawyer, and everything went very smoothly. He seemed
keen to get the deal settled as soon as possible, which is
why there was no haggling. I told them the price that I
wanted, and he had agreed to it straight away. I don't
know why he was so keen on my property, but I do know
that the estate agent said he'd been given a contract to
find exactly that sort of property – one with lots of small
flats inside – and he could get me a very good price.

'I think that must have been his plan; to have some
kind of commune built in there for his families, both
those above and those below. It's an incredible thing for
me to think really, that I did business with, shook the
hand of and took the money earned by, a man who did
such terrible things.'

Was this indeed one of Fritzl's fantasies? Everyone
living happily ever after – the privileged, school-going,

vitamin-enriched children who lived with him and Rosi, and the malnourished, pasty-faced, hunched dwellers of the netherworld? Did Fritzl's imagination truly know no bounds?

However much he fancied the idea of providing for the extended clan, living happily ever after like some dysfunctional Von Trapp dynasty, cash was always going to be a crucial factor in his old age. He received €900 a week in benefits for raising the three cellar children, and he had state and work pensions of €4,000 per month. The properties he owned, or upon which he owed money, numbered eight in all at the time he was arrested.

A detailed financial trawl of his real-estate empire for this book has discovered that in 1979, presumably for tax purposes, he signed over the Ybbsstrasse family home to his eldest daughter, Ulrike. Then, in 1986, it changed hands once more, this time being registered lock, stock and barrel with his wife Rosemarie. It changes hands a final time in 1998 when Fritzl is registered once more as the sole owner. The deal was concluded in September of that year and comprises the main house of 721 square metres but with outbuildings spanning a further 346 square metres. A second deal on the same day is for the same address and covers 282 square metres. It relates to further outbuildings on a strip of land that borders the rear of the house and is also owned by Fritzl.

In July, 2002, records show that he purchased property on the Waidhofnerstrasse in Amstetten covering a total of 1,416 square metres that included a separate detached house in the grounds spanning 283 square metres. In

December, 2004, he purchased the Linzer Strasse property, a sprawling complex that also spreads out to cover another plot on the Julius Raab Promenade in St Poelten and covering a total of 1,081 square metres. Both sites have commercial and residential letting status.

On 29 September, 2006, he signed a deal on the property at 1 Strasse 10b in Kematen covering a total of 388 square metres, including a separate building on the ground covering 253 square metres. In November the following year he purchased Ybbsitzerstrasse 108 in Waidhofen an der Ybbs, a property covering a total of 1,110 square metres. Fritzl owned the Gasthof Seestern at the Mondsee lake until he sold it in 1996. In 2008 he bought another rental property at 1 Strasse 10a in Kematen for €500,000.

All these houses required enormous maintenance in terms of caretakers, property taxes, upkeep, cleaning. He often hired people on the black market to avoid paying the high employer's costs in Austria. He also used the clearly complex financial morass he found himself in as an excuse to retreat to the cellar to 'do the books'. Which he sometimes did, when not up to more nefarious pursuits within its confines.

So far so scheming. But in 2006, 2007 and 2008 he took out loans against the properties of €3,879,500. Where did this money go? He told the bank it was for renovations and for a business at the Ybbsstrasse address dealing with underwear. The proprietor of the firm was duly listed on the Internet as one Josef Fritzl. And yet, when police raided the property, there was no trace of any underwear firm.

He did make some renovations, and he started to

develop some of his land. But was the rest being kept by
Fritzl for one final, grand roll of the dice? A trust fund
for the children . . . or the down payment for a swift cab
ride, a plane ticket and a shack somewhere in the back of
beyond in Thailand? Detectives in Amstetten, seeking to
unravel the enormity of Fritzl's crimes, have called on the
services of a special finance section of the national police
in Vienna to trawl through the labyrinthine financial
morass. The rents from his tenants – six in the Linzer
Strasse house alone – are still going into his bank account
but are now administered by his lawyer. Those funds not
used to service his debts will go towards the cost of
defending him at his trial. And there is every likelihood
of lawsuits on behalf of the cellar family to seize whatever
is left, both cash and real estate, to pay towards the costs
of extended therapy.

At the time of his arrest Fritzl was drawing in around
€15,000 a month in rents – but he had mortgage outgoings
on the Ybbsstrasse address and other houses, and had
large borrowings to service. He had complained to Hoera
of feeling the pinch at various times, invariably paying
cash, as he had with the Seestern guest house, for his new
properties and often leaving himself short.

The friend recalls: 'Yes, money was a worry to him. He
said he was frantic he wouldn't have enough to, as he put
it, "see me through". He once said: "I remember growing
up and we didn't have enough and I made a vow to
myself that I would always have some coal in my trousers.
I don't want to skimp on my last days. Besides, I've got
responsibilities, a lot of kids to look after." In the last
year he said he'd taken to doing the Lotto at weekends,

which was out of character for him. He was a stingy guy with money and spending 12 euros on a Friday for the Saturday draw was a big step for him. It would've pained him so he must have been hurting on the financial front.'

Money worries at various stages are thought to have lain behind a series of mystery blazes at the Ybbsstrasse house at a time when Elisabeth had spent almost 20 years underground and given birth to seven children. On 22 August, 2003, a fire broke out in one of the rental flats on the ground floor. Fritzl discovered the fire approximately ten minutes after it started. He told firemen: 'I smelled smoke, raced downstairs and kicked in the door to the flat and faced a wall of smoke. My son Josef had also come to help; he smashed the kitchen window. I rushed inside and rescued Annemarie, the tenant, who was motionless on the floor.' She was taken to hospital suffering from smoke inhalation, although she later recovered. The fire was investigated by police and eventually Fritzl received €10,000 compensation from his insurance company.

Within a year it happened again when the power meter on the ground floor caught fire. Once again, the omnipresent Josef Fritzl just happened to be the one who discovered it. This time the insurance company blamed a rat gnawing through the power cable as the culprit and Fritzl pocketed a further €1,000. Then, on 26 December, 2004, at around 9.30 a.m., a TV in the children's playroom caught fire. The TV was destroyed and in the process some furniture, toys and a PlayStation went up in smoke. Again Josef Fritzl extinguished the fire, and the insurance company paid €3,000. This was a man who had a criminal record as a rapist and was under suspicion of torching his own guest house years earlier. But just as no neighbours joined the dots during Elisabeth's martyrdom, so no officials thought something was amiss in the Fritzl household.

Vienna-based insurance agent Peter Stoecker believes: 'For someone to have three fires on their property in this space of time is extremely suspicious and, statistically, it is highly unlikely to be an accident on every occasion. I would have expected a police investigation. I understand he was once looked at for arson, but of course, as he wasn't convicted, that was probably not recorded anywhere any more.'

By the end of June, 2008, the money detectives had determined one thing: Fritzl budgeted the equivalent of £200 a month for the needs of all the cellar dwellers, putting them firmly among the 5 per cent of Austrians classified as living below the national poverty line. He bought meat and milk whose use-by dates were about to expire, frozen food that had lived longer in ice than it had done in field or sea, generic tinned goods, knock-down clothes, and unscented soaps and shampoo. He even provided Elisabeth with a little gizmo that attaches to the bottom of a tube of toothpaste and is rolled upwards to extract every last scrap. He had no repairs to attend to below ground, no cinema tickets to buy for them, no outings to arrange or holidays to pay for. And still he made his secret family a low-cost tribe. He documented his outgoings in a little invoice book, each month chronicled in order, the neat rows of figures masking a plethora of silent suffering.

While Fritzl pondered, the family below existed but did not thrive. Elisabeth would have had to strive every day to try to stimulate the children as they grew older. Their bafflement at their incarceration must have increased with each new TV programme they saw. Be it daytime soap or night-time documentary, they must have become more and more anxious to know why they had to spend their lives in a concrete cube. She could never have asked them what their dreams were, because she could never fulfil them; she could not ask them what they wished for, because the wishes could never come true. The ultimate cruelty of Fritzl's prison was that it robbed his charges of hope. While Elisabeth could infuse them with love, she could not give them hope because that would have been one more lie among the millions he heaped upon them.

Such is the pride and arrogance of Josef Fritzl that it never once registered on his radar that the products of an unnatural relationship kept artificially underground in a cruel satire of normality would require medical attention, perhaps lasting their entire lives, to ever bring them close to becoming 'normal' people if he chose to set them free. In all the interviews with his lawyer and with police he has never once acknowledged that what he did might have been detrimental to the mental and physical health of those he professed to love.

For a man of precision and planning, he may have been growing feeble in those last months as he dreamed of a rose-tinted future where the Fritzl offspring lived together in peace and harmony. Certainly his memory seems to have become impaired in the 12 months before everything ended. Lifeguard Johannes Hoffmann met Fritzl several times a week when he went swimming at the local baths. Fritzl would swim 20 lengths – exercise which he boasted kept him in shape 'for the ladies'.

Hoffmann recalls: 'I used to speak to him at the side of the pool. Most of the time we spoke about chess; he was really interested in the game. He once said: "It's a long game, chess, a game of strategy and patience." He used to ask me about my chess computer and wanted me to show it to him. He'd be interested in trying it out, he said. At first he gave the impression of being a really relaxed and peaceful person and not nervous or danger-ous in any way. But last year I noticed that things started to slip his mind. When he stopped in the water to chat with me he'd ask a question – and then, not 30 seconds later, he'd be asking it again. His memory really seemed to be fading. He appeared to be a man under pressure, preoccupied all the time, which I thought rather odd given his age and the fact that I thought he should be enjoying the twilight years of his life. I think I asked him about his family a couple of times and I distinctly remember him telling me he was divorced, which was another lie of course.'

Of course. It was what Josef Fritzl did best. But things were about to change for ever.

8. Earthquake

Elisabeth had lost track of how long Kerstin had been sick. For days she lay on her bed, her body growing sicker and sicker. She had fits that her mother and Stefan tried to ease by putting a piece of cloth-wrapped wood in her mouth. Little Felix cried as she bit her lips in torment until they bled. Sweat poured from her body, soaking the mattress. The cellar air was growing ever poorer as the ancient ventilator system struggled to cope. In their isolation her pain was magnified, reverberating off the walls, echoing into every corner of the chamber. Elisabeth had nursed her children through many crises during the years; nothing had ever been this bad.

What she knew of hospitals and medicine was confined to the pregnancy books supplied by her jailer and the American soap *ER* that played on the TV. Fritzl's idea of medication was aspirin, and sometimes cough medicine. He had seen Kerstin in her agony, made a point of breaking his routine to enter the secret familial chamber every day to gauge for himself how she was faring. He admitted to himself that things did not look good. His first-born illegitimate child, the cornerstone of the secret tribe, was growing weaker by the second.

He had to be careful, he knew. He must have weighed up in his diseased mind the pros and cons of action and inaction. His plot to bring them back into society was still crystallizing; to seek out proper medical attention ran the risk of exposure. Down here, in the darkness, his word was law; in the land above, his power was limited.

Mad or bad, Fritzl ultimately knew that no one would understand the separate realm he ruled. To allow Kerstin to be seen by a doctor would inevitably provoke questions which might prove embarrassing, not to say lethal, to his scheme. In his twin lives, both public and secret, he had always experienced an overriding need to keep the illusion of respectability intact. Now, in the half-light, his mind churned like the cheap washing machine in the corner of the cellar, going over and over; what to do, what to do, what to do?

Kerstin had suffered erratic fits almost since birth, probably as a result of the inherited genes of her father/ grandfather. Broadly speaking, inbreeding passes on 'bad genes', compounding and magnifying their effects in an inbred child. 'Close genetic relatives run the risk of having offspring who have a reduced chance of surviving,' says genetic expert Debra Lieberman of the University of Hawaii.

DNA – the blueprint of life – is divided up into two sets of 23 chromosomes for a total of 46 in the average human being. One set of 23 comes from the father, while the other set comes from the mother. What the scientists call a 'deleterious' gene, and the layperson knows as 'bad', is usually counteracted by one from either parent. Lieberman explains: 'The good version acts like a back-up, effectively preventing disease the bad gene might have caused.' But having a child with your own daughter drastically increases the chances of getting two copies of the deleterious gene as compared to fathering a child with someone outside your family. 'Each of you would have a copy of that bad gene, so there's a good chance the child won't have a normal copy to work with.'

Multiply that by any other deleterious genes sprinkled among an estimated 50,000 active genes in humans, and there are bound to be some life-shortening problems. Fritzl had never taken such science on board during his long reign of horror. As for Kerstin's alarming ill health, he simply hoped the fits would pass, as they had passed before. But this time he wasn't so sure. Inaction, if it led to her death, would create its own unique problems.

He wasn't worried about any rebellion from Elisabeth; he had long since ceased to care about her emotional needs and wants. Any dissent over his demands and routine could soon be beaten out of her. No, what most concerned him now was how to dispose of a body should Kerstin's illness prove fatal. She was no baby Michael, a shrivelled, helpless, almost weightless creature just 72 hours old. Fritzl had hauled tons of earth from this cavern, but that was 15 years ago and he wasn't getting any younger. Besides, an adult body was a different matter; he knew it would never fit into the maw of the house's central heating furnace.

Tick tock. The cheap alarm clock next to Elisabeth's bed was like a metronome counting down the minutes as Fritzl mulled over his increasingly limited options. Did he love Kerstin? He certainly loved the notion of her. He loved being the centre of attention as she respectfully called him 'grandfather' and he recited tales of the world he decreed she should never see. He loved keeping her captive, loved her resemblance to the daughter he coveted and then took, loved the whole warped idea of pulling the wool over the eyes of an unwitting public. But real love was an emotion he was incapable of feeling.

Equilibrium – that was what he sought in his covert world. Everything on an even keel. This sickness, which seemed to grow steadily worse from the morning of Tuesday, 15 April, 2008, was a threat to the order, discipline and obedience of the cellar and its dwellers. He didn't like it because he couldn't control it.

Tick tock. By Thursday Kerstin was slipping in and out of consciousness. Cold compresses on her forehead and thighs did little to bring down her temperature. She could no longer walk to the toilet and was fouling her bed. She began to talk in her sleep, thrashing around in her fever. Her lips looked as if she had been beaten. A grey fluid wept from her eyes and spittle ran in rivulets from her mouth. The aspirin clearly wasn't having any effect. Elisabeth told her tormentor that Kerstin must go to hospital, that otherwise she would die.

The rapid change in Kerstin changed Elisabeth too. She seemed to grow stronger as her daughter grew weaker. Her whole life underground had been one of subservience; she placed her morality, feelings, hopes, aspirations and emotions into spiritual cryonic suspension, acceding to her brutal father's whims on every occasion. She did it at first to avoid being beaten; later she did it for her children. Fritzl, who never worried a jot about some Spartacus-like slave rebellion in his underworld, noticed the change in her as she sat and comforted her child. It was as if he could read her mind, a mind which said, 'If she dies, then it's all over for you.'

Kurt Kletzer, the Viennese psychotherapist who constructed a profile of Fritzl in his formative years for this book, explains: 'He would have sensed that she wouldn't be the pliable servant that she'd been in the past. She lived for her children, particularly her first child. She was her rock and her salvation, her best friend and her ally. If she had died, the weight in this uneven contest would have shifted inexorably and he was seeing the first signs of those tectonic plates moving. Fritzl could still rape her. Yes, he could still keep her and Stefan and Felix prisoner. But his profound need for respect, for esteem among his secret tribe would be lost for ever. As Elisabeth pleaded for him to get medical help, he would have marked the steel in her voice and it would have unnerved him.'

Tick tock. The enormity of the dilemma facing Fritzl was a torment.

'Give it one more day,' he said on the Friday of that week, as if he was hoping for a miracle cure, when really he was clawing to find a way out.

There was supreme irony in this; he was now a prisoner of the monstrous edifice which he had created all those years ago. Everything in his life so far had been a calculated step; the continued life, or impending death, of his first-born incest child was one more piece in his mosaic of deceit, and he knew he had to get it right. As Elisabeth, Stefan and Felix sought to give Kerstin comfort on the night of 18 April, Josef Fritzl slipped into his single room at the top of the house and went to sleep with the seeds of a cunning plan already forming. As the young woman deteriorated still further, her immune system shutting down as a result of her years of imprisonment, he was asleep within minutes, satisfied that he had got it right.

Neither Fritzl nor Elisabeth knew then that the clock ticking down on their daughter's life was also marking the end of the cellar tribe's long and painful underground existence.

On Saturday morning came the familiar rumble as the last door to the cave opened. It was 8,516 days since Elisabeth had been tricked into entering this place – drugged, imprisoned and then subject to abuse on an unparalleled scale. Broken down it amounted to 204,384 pain-filled hours as her life ebbed away like sand in an egg timer. How she managed to live through her captivity in the cellar is beyond the comprehension of most people. She was convinced she would die within its fungal walls, hoping against hope that some spark of humanity would reignite in her father and he would spare her children and one day let them free.

Fritzl asked how Kerstin was this morning; the young woman was conscious on Elisabeth's bed but doubled up in pain with severe cramps. She was clutching her stomach, moaning in agony. Fritzl peered at her, then moved away to sit at the little table where he held his obscene 'family' chats with the cellar occupants. He produced a pen and paper, then told Elisabeth to write the following:

Wednesday, I gave her aspirin and cough medicine for the condition. Thursday, the cough worsened. Friday, the coughing got

*even worse. She has been biting her lip as well as her tongue.
Please, please help her! Kerstin is really terrified of other people,
she's never been in a hospital. If there are any problems, please
ask my father for help, he is the only person that she knows.*

In a single line underneath the mother added:

*Kerstin – please stay strong, until we see each other again! We
will come back to you soon!*

The illusion of Elisabeth's life as a runaway in some
cult that no one had ever heard of – an illusion that no
one had seen fit to question – was to be performed one
more time. Elisabeth then wrapped the half-conscious
Kerstin in a blanket and, together with Stefan, helped
carry her undernourished daughter, who weighed just
50kg, through the cellar portal to her father's car upstairs.

'What about mother?' asked Elisabeth.

'Your mother is away,' said Fritzl. Ever the meticulous
planner, he knew Rosemarie would not walk in on their
exit from the cellar; she was at a safe distance, on holiday
in Italy.

Elisabeth struggled through the exit to the cellar,
through the maze of doors which guarded the route to it
and out into the light of day. It was the first time she had
seen sunlight since 1984 and she was temporarily blinded.
For Stefan, it was the first time ever that he had seen a
world beyond the walls of the cellar. The senses of both
mother and son drank in this brave new world – a world
she had long ago left behind and he had never experienced. There was the smell of grass, the sound of a

motorbike, the vapour trail of a plane high in the sky, the tang of apple blossom in the air. They saw the swimming pool Fritzl had added, the building of which had been used as a cover for the earth tunnelled out to extend their prison, and Elisabeth noticed the other changes her industrious father had made to the property.

But it was only fleeting, if tangible, contact with a previous life, and one that paled beside her fears for her daughter. It was also over as soon as it had begun; mother and son were immediately taken back into the cellar. Back they went through the entryway, and the door once more closed behind them.

Felix was seriously distressed at the sudden disappearance of his mother and brother and asked where they were and what was happening to them 'outside the door'. Elisabeth had long ago told him there was no world beyond that door; now she had to fabricate a new story, saying that Kerstin had to leave to get better, but that she would be back soon.

'Nothing will split us up,' she said. She hoped. But fear about Kerstin's dire condition gnawed away at her.

Above ground Fritzl picked up his telephone and dialled 144, the Austrian 999 for medical assistance.

'This is an emergency,' he said. 'I've just found my granddaughter unconscious.' Fritzl thought he was being as clever as always. In actuality, with that phone call, he made the down payment on the reckoning with justice that he so richly deserved.

'I found her in the hallway,' he said when the ambulance arrived. 'I put her on to the back seat of the car to make her comfortable.'

The note he had dictated to his daughter he kept in his pocket; he would produce it later. He then tidied up some things in his flat and drove to the hospital to assume the mantle of caring grandfather. The lie was to be that, after years of leaving newborn children on his doorstep, the prodigal daughter had returned one last time to deposit a chronically sick young woman into his care. Look! She even wrote a note about it!

This time, however, things were to go badly wrong for the master illusionist. He may have fooled social workers, building inspectors, his wife, his family, his neighbours and his upstairs children. But he could not fool Dr Albert Reiter.

Dr Reiter, the head of the intensive care unit at the Amstetten Hospital, was staggered at the condition of the young woman. She had slipped into unconsciousness in the ambulance. Kerstin was showing the signs of suffering a total shutdown of her vital organs. Kidneys and liver were malfunctioning, she had a high temperature, her breathing was strained, one lung partially filled with fluid. She was placed on the critically ill list within minutes of arrival.

But it was her appearance that evoked the most curiosity in the doctor; the pallor of her skin, the thinness of her arms, the presence of anaemia, the total lack of dental work, her bleeding gums, her missing teeth. If he didn't know better, he would have said the young woman looked as if she had never seen a ray of sunshine in her life.

A hospital worker later told the media: 'She was like a phantom lying in bed. She was a rarity in the modern world – an unknown citizen. There was no medical history, no paperwork – and you know how much we Austrians like paperwork – she looked as if she had never seen a doctor. In fact, she just looked terrible. We were staring at an enigma.'

As Kerstin was stabilized, including being put into an artificial coma and linked to a dialysis machine, her blood and stomach screened for poison but no traces found, Dr Reiter was telephoned from reception and informed that a man had arrived with information about the new patient.

Dr Reiter recalled later: 'I met the man and he produced a note saying he was the grandfather of this patient. It was one hour after her admission. The note said that this woman was called Kerstin and was in a very bad condition, and the mother asked us to help her. She told us that she had a headache and had taken some drugs for the headache but nothing more. The note said she took one pill, and then she got dizzy and then she got convulsions. And then the convulsions came hourly and then she was brought to hospital by ambulance. The man rang the ambulance when he found her and the ambulance brought her to hospital.

'My impression was that he was a correct man. He said that his daughter, the mother of our patient, lived away from home but that she had brought the daughter to his house. The man, Fritzl, asked us to do everything we could for Kerstin. He was a very polite and normal man but there was something about his tone I didn't like. It made me think that something wasn't right.

'What made me particularly suspicious was that he didn't seem to think it important to answer any of my

16. Rosemarie Fritzl and a family friend in Mondsee, Austria.

17. Josef Fritzl during a four-week holiday in Pataya, Thailand, from 1 January to 3 February 1998. Despite being without any of his family members, he bought children's clothes and lingerie while there.

18. Josef Fritzl (*centred, behind the man in the blue shirt*) during his four-week holiday in Pataya, Thailand.

19. Staff at this Linz brothel told of how Josef Fritzl was a client of theirs and was violent towards the girls who worked there.

20. Aerial view of the Amstetten Mauer hospital, where the cellar family have lived since being freed from 40 Ybbsstrasse.

21. The house that was converted for visiting doctors of the cellar family to share at the Amstetten Mauer hospital, complete with a secret garden.

22. The window to Josef Fritzl's cell (*centre*) at the St Poelten prison, where he is currently in custody.

23. The waitress Diana Arwanis who served Josef Fritzl and his family every Sunday at the Pizza Casa Verona: 'They always had the same table, the kids were not allowed to speak.'

24. Elisabeth's best friend from school, Christa Woldrich, who has now made a CD for her pal.

EXPERIENCE & Christa

24 JAHRE
Elisabeth F.

25. Despite Christa's good intentions, Elisabeth's lawyers decided that the CD was not in their client's best interests and ordered sales to be stopped.

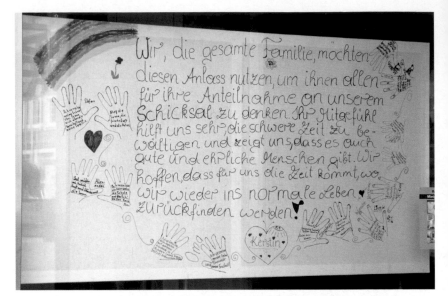

26. The banner that the Fritzl children made to thank the local community for their support throughout the investigation. It was hung in the window of a local shopping centre.

27. As the world's media gathered in Amstetten to ask why the town had seen nothing of Elisabeth during her twenty-four years underground, locals staged a rally to show their support for the cellar survivors.

28. The 17-year-old Martina Posch, who was sexually assaulted and murdered twenty-two years ago near the lake Mondsee, where Austrian incest father Josef Fritzl had owned a house. Fritzl was investigated as a possible suspect, but he had an alibi.

29. Julia Kuehrer, who was reported missing and whose case has been reopened by police to see if there is any link to the sexual predator Josef Fritzl.

30. Amstetten officials at a press conference that was called in the days after the cellar family case emerged to discuss the latest developments. From left to right: Klaus Schwertner, spokesman for the Lower Austrian hospitals; Amstetten doctors Albert Reiter and Berthold Kepplinger, who cared for the cellar family; Christoph Herbst, lawyer to Elisabeth Fritzl.

31. Austrian artist and theologist Florian Naehrer sparked outrage after putting up a picture of Josef Fritzl in a local café to show that 'God sees good in every person'. The acrylic, costing £1,200, is on display in the café of a bookstore in St Poelten.

questions about the wider background, like the fact there were no medical records – she didn't seem to exist. He simply demanded we make Kerstin better so that he could take her away again. I told him that the girl was in a very bad condition, that she had to be placed on a ventilator. I told him that any care we could give her was hampered by the fact that we had absolutely no medical records for her, no record of a GP, no medical history, nothing.

'I was suspicious about the note. I couldn't believe that the mother of a seriously ill 19-year-old girl would simply offload her at the hospital and disappear. From the tone of the letter the mother had sent, it was clear that she cared very deeply for her child. So why wasn't she here?'

The attitude of the doctor was something that Fritzl, the manipulator and deceiver par excellence, was ill prepared for. His attitude was threatening, posturing. 'Just get her better, doctor, and I'll take care of the rest.' He walked out of the door, returning several times over the weekend for updates on her condition.

Dr Reiter was puzzled and confused. 'I was certain of only one thing, that the mother was the only one who could help,' he said. 'I contacted the grandfather again, and told him we desperately needed to speak to the mother. I was convinced she had information that was the key to the mystery illness. I couldn't understand why he was so reluctant to help, but he did agree.'

Fritzl said he would 'try to find' Elisabeth, telling Dr Reiter the phoney cover story that he had fabricated about the cult.

Dr Reiter asked the hospital's public relations department to put out an appeal to the local media and even got Fritzl to provide a photograph of Elisabeth as a teenager before she joined the 'cult'. Dr Reiter also gave out his personal mobile number so that anyone with information could get in touch.

There was another call made. It was to Amstetten police station from the hospital, saying a most curious emergency case had turned up. The police were on to Fritzl from this moment on. The call came through at 10.37 a.m., from the Mostviertel Amstetten State Hospital to report the admission of a mysterious 'female person'. The patient was 'unresponsive and in a critical condition', and her symptoms suggested that she had been severely neglected. The man accompanying the woman was one Josef Fritzl, of Ybbsstrasse 40, Amstetten.

Franz Polzer, a serious and correct man, a family man, a police officer of many years' standing, heard about the delivery of Kerstin to the hospital later that day. As head of the State Criminal Office for the region covering Amstetten he was aware of the numerous babies that had turned up unannounced on the Fritzl doorstep down the years. This was number four – and she was no baby.

In an exclusive interview for this book he said: 'My first thought, and that of the other detectives, was, "Whoever left this person must have had help." This was no baby weighing a few pounds. Simple, but logical; she couldn't have been left there on her own by just one person.'

When journalists from the local newspaper arrived at Fritzl's house, expecting his cooperation in the appeal, they were stunned to be turned away. One recalls: 'I was shocked. Instead of being the concerned father I expected, he told me to clear off. He was shouting and swearing and really furious. He said he'd wanted nothing to do with the appeal, but that the "bloody doctor" had forced him into it.'

Fritzl's mind was working overtime. His options were narrowing; his two distinct worlds were on a dangerous collision course. Although he toyed with the idea of freeing the cellar family, he knew the risks he ran of exposure. Captives would say or do almost anything if they thought they were going to be freed. But once that freedom was gained, all bets were off. Fritzl enjoyed his life. He juggled his debts, visited his prostitutes, went on his foreign holidays. He had the respect – or at least the obedience – of his upstairs children with Rosemarie, and of the incest children below. Fritzl was not a martyr; he did not want his world to end. So he reasoned that, if he kept Elisabeth locked up and gave her updates about Kerstin's condition, all would be well.

It would not. The earthquake was about to hit Amstetten.

The warning rumbles came on the night of Saturday, 19 April. The news report that evening on the local TV station flashed up a picture of Elisabeth as a teenager. Fritzl felt his mouth go dry as he watched the broadcast.

Does anybody know where this woman is? Detectives have made an appeal for a 42-year-old woman, Elisabeth Fritzl, who is believed to be somewhere in the Amstetten area to urgently contact the hospital in Amstetten. Her 19-year-old daughter is in a life-threatening condition and the doctors need urgent

information about the circumstances of her illness in
order to be able to treat her. Anyone who knows where
Elisabeth Fritzl is keeping herself or where her daughter
resides is asked to contact the police immediately.

The news report repeated the old lies about Elisabeth
being in a sect, a cult, told how she had already abandoned
three children on her parents' doorstep. Unbeknown to
Fritzl, the report had also been broadcast on the radio
and was being picked up by the national media.

'Contact the police immediately' – this was something
Fritzl had not envisaged. He thought the appeal would
be limited to a broadcast for help from the hospital.
Now this meant more questions, perhaps ones even he
couldn't conjure up answers to. He didn't know that
officers, investigating child abandonment and child neglect charges against Elisabeth, were already forming a
squad to look for her on their own; they had his faked
letters from down the years and were already in contact
with cult and sect specialists who might be able to shed
light on where Elisabeth had gone. All enquiries quickly
turned into dead ends because in a country as small as
Austria, the number of such groups could be counted on
two hands.

Manfred Wohlfahrt, a priest with the St Poelten diocese
who tracks cults and sects, made the observation to
officers that it might have been better if they had contacted him in 1984 when Elisabeth first went missing. No
one ever had. Those sects that he did put them in touch
with now were cooperating with the police; none wanted
to be linked with a demented breeder who dropped her

children off on doorsteps in the dead of night. Nor did they know anyone of Elisabeth's age who might have done such things.

Fritzl, quite rightly, had the feeling that things were spinning out of control; perhaps letting Kerstin die might have been a better option after all. Also unbeknown to him was the fact that the news report had been seen by Elisabeth, Stefan and Felix in the cellar below him. All were stunned into silence, a terrible fear gripping them that Kerstin might die. Elisabeth felt more powerless in the moments following the broadcast than she had ever felt before. 'Only her mother can help us,' said the doctor in the white coat with the nice manner and kind face. Her father had never let her leave this terrible prison, except to help move Kerstin outside. She knew she had to see her daughter, but what could she expect from a man with an iceberg for a heart?

Elisabeth had begged her father many times, at the beginning of her imprisonment, to free her, but all to no avail. What could make him change his mind now? A colossal determination was building inside her as the authorities, duped into apathy and indolence for 24 years, were finally launching an investigation – a long-overdue investigation that included an interview with Josef Fritzl of Ybbsstrasse 40.

'I was upstairs in the flat when I suddenly heard noises in the stairwell,' he lied in an interview with detectives who were waiting at the hospital for him when he went to visit Kerstin on Sunday. 'I went to investigate and saw this young woman leaning apathetically against one wall. She looked to be in a terrible state and she was carrying a note. It said that her name was Kerstin and that she urgently needed medical attention.

'My daughter Elisabeth must have sent her. She went off her rocker years ago, ran away and we've never seen her since. She must have gone further downhill. Years back, she dropped kids off at my doorstep and my wife and I raised them as our own – it was the least we could do. But she must be in some state to let her daughter get like that, huh?'

Ever the fluent storyteller, he produced another letter, the way a magician pulls rabbits from a top hat, intended to reinforce the lies. It was a note he had made Elisabeth write in January 2008. In it she had written that her son Felix had been very ill in September, and that he had had epileptic seizures and symptoms of paralysis, but had recovered. Kerstin, the letter read, had also had health problems, including circulatory disorders, and stabbing chest pains. But, it continued, Elisabeth, Stefan and Felix would soon be coming home, and perhaps they would even be able to celebrate their birthdays together.

This was to be a fundamental part of his story *if* he chose to let the cellar children and Elisabeth free. Now it was used to bolster the old lies as he wriggled and squirmed to try to keep the police away from his home at all costs. The police later admitted they had suspicions about Fritzl, as had Dr Reiter. But the letter was something tangible. For a very short while, it succeeded in throwing them off the scent.

The letter bore the postmark of Kematen an der Krems, 70 kilometres from Amstetten. Fritzl had posted it to himself while out on a shopping trip for the cellar clan. Naturally, none of the doctors questioned in the Kematen vicinity had any recollection of a woman named Kerstin. The police became increasingly perplexed. Did this mysterious sect even exist? Father Wohlfahrt was then shown Elisabeth's letter from January, the note penned about Kerstin's sickness, and the note that Kerstin had been carrying. Did the letters offer any clues as to where the woman who wrote them could be, the police asked? Did the diction and choice of words suggest a sect? Wohlfahrt studied the blue letters, written in a handwriting that looked like calligraphy, assembled into 'oddly smooth, constructed and not very authentic' sentences; the letters seemed 'dictated'. Wohlfahrt said: 'There is no evidence of a sect.'

The police decided to switch their focus to Amstetten in general – and Josef Fritzl in particular. Colonel Polzer explains: 'We had him in our sights. By Monday or Tuesday of the following week – I can't recall the exact timetable – we were thinking that perhaps the children who had been abandoned by Elisabeth over the years on the Fritzl doorstep were from different fathers. So we decided on a DNA test for all the family – Fritzl, the children upstairs, Kerstin and Rosemarie. Only Fritzl refused. "I have no time," he said. Of course this behaviour only made him more suspicious.

'The DNA tests came back before the weekend. The tests stated that it seemed highly probable that Josef Fritzl was the father of Kerstin as well as the children who were abandoned on the doorstep. But they couldn't say so with certainty without the DNA of Fritzl himself.'

The police pondered their next move. And Fritzl pondered his.

He next came to the cellar on Tuesday, but it was as a different character than the domineering patriarch demanding obedience, respect or sex. He was furtive and tired; plainly he had not slept well.

'I saw it,' said Elisabeth, before he could speak, referring to the news broadcast. 'We all did. I must go to her, Papa. You heard what they said, I must go to her.'

Fritzl sat down at the little table. Stefan and Felix looked at him intently. He rubbed his face with his hands. 'I don't know, I don't know . . . the doctors are doing all they can, you must know that.'

This time, for the first time in her whole life, with her teeth rotted and her hair white, the looks and vibrancy of her youth squandered in a place where only mushrooms should have thrived, Elisabeth stood before her jailer and thought she might be on the verge of some breakthrough. She had made deals, with herself, with him, to make her existence bearable down the years. She felt powerless when she heard of her daughter's plight on the television; now she sensed the power shift in this most unequal of relationships, a movement in the dynamics of their master–mistress roles. Fritzl's half-baked whimsy of releasing them all came back to him again and it suddenly struck him that, if he could exact silence, then maybe it might work.

Elisabeth did not let up. She begged her father, down on her knees, but she didn't cry. Tears never did any good in his presence; besides, she had done all her crying for Kerstin. She just knew she had to get out of the cellar.

Fritzl, in his heart, knew it too. But still he stalled for time, trying to organize his jumbled thoughts about freedom into a viable scheme. Before he got up he agreed that Elisabeth could visit Kerstin in the hospital: but there would be conditions. And it would not happen today. She had won, but she was still captive – and her daughter still desperately ill.

She did not know that the police were now engaged in a full-scale hunt for her. Elisabeth was still listed as a missing person; now she was also moving into the frame as a criminal. If Kerstin was to die, as seemed highly probable in those first days of treatment, Elisabeth would be guilty of extreme abuse and child neglect. The police were more interested in catching a criminal than a runaway girl. Herr Polzer admits: 'It's true that Elisabeth was initially wanted for child neglect of a most serious order.'

Fritzl also worried that even at this late stage forensic tests might have spotted his saliva on the envelope or the stamp, which would have incriminated him as the sender of the letters. He had to put the police off the scent.

Against the backdrop of his increasingly diminishing options Fritzl had made up his mind to allow Elisabeth and the other children out of the cellar at the weekend to visit Kerstin. His wife was still away in Italy with the other half of his incest tribe but he telephoned her to say Elisabeth had arrived home, unexpectedly. 'What a miracle!' he lied. Rosemarie and the upstairs children hurried back.

But more important even than his bluff, he had to get Elisabeth to rehearse her lines; he still valued his liberty, remembering with some discomfort his prison experience from years before. He told himself that he could pull it off – he always had done, hadn't he?

At some point on Friday, 25 April Fritzl returned and, with his trusty remote control which he kept in a drawer in the final workroom before the cellar entrance, he led Elisabeth back into the world of light. Stefan and Felix accompanied her into an environment the older boy had barely glimpsed and his younger brother had never before seen. Back rolled the door, click went the locks on the other seven and soon, struggling to walk after a lifetime in the cramped cellar, Fritzl led his secret family upstairs to an existence that the children had been told was a fantasy.

'On the Friday when he let them out,' says Polzer, 'we had obtained a court order demanding that he submit to a DNA test. He gave one in the afternoon but we didn't know its results until the following week.'

In one room of his apartment, surrounded by pictures of the children she had borne him and the siblings she had lost touch with 24 years ago in a previous life, Fritzl dictated his terms to Elisabeth and his cavern children. She must say, when they arrived at the hospital, that she had come back from the sect to help her daughter; that she didn't know where Kerstin lived and was shocked at her condition. She had brought her to her parents' home because she didn't know who else to turn to; she could not be held responsible for her condition because Kerstin was a grown woman and she had lost contact with her some years before. She was to say nothing of the cellar or the fictional whereabouts of her other children, mentioned in the letter Fritzl had made her write back in

January. 'You are there to sort out the medical treatment for Kerstin and then you are to leave.'

What did Rosemarie make of this apparition before her, her ravaged daughter and her equally ravaged children? What flashed through her mind, as she was told to wait with the children while Fritzl went with Elisabeth to the hospital in a bid to underwrite his fiction one last time? Was this when she realized that she had been living a lie for over half a century? Or was it in the small hours when the seismic shocks began to ripple out from Amstetten, to amaze and astound the rest of the world? Rosemarie, the long-suffering wife, was left with the diminished cellar children on her sofa – and tried to make sense of it all.

'I have no idea, frankly, what Rosemarie made of all this, of suddenly being confronted with her daughter after all these years, and the grandchildren she never knew she had,' says Polzer. 'I can only assume that Fritzl made all sorts of threats to them, to Elisabeth and the children, to make them keep silent about where they had really come from. It must have been quite a strange reunion . . .'

On Saturday evening, 26 April, 2008, Fritzl told Elisabeth to put on her coat. It was at this point that he made his biggest mistake – a telephone call to the hospital before they left. 'Elisabeth has returned. I'm bringing her to the hospital and she wants to see her daughter. We don't want any trouble – do not call the police.'

But for the hospital it was too much – Fritzl had overplayed his hand, and medical staff made the call he had tried so hard to prevent.

The earthquake began.

*

'We received two phone calls that evening,' says Herr Polzer. 'One was to say that the girl's mother was on the way to the hospital. Then we received another to say that she'd arrived there. Police officers were despatched . . .'

If it occurred to Fritzl that his daughter might look like a suitable case for treatment herself, he gave no indication. He led her through to the intensive care ward where Dr Reiter was waiting. Not unnaturally, the doctor was stunned at the sight of her white hair, the same sallow skin as her daughter. She was thin and had difficulty forming words as she struggled with obvious pain in her mouth – the result of years of untreated tooth decay.

Dr Reiter was concerned that, when he asked her questions, it was her father who always tried to butt in to answer them for her. The doctor asked where Kerstin had been living and Elisabeth was forced to say she didn't know. It became clear to Reiter that he was being fobbed off with half-truths if not outright lies. Elisabeth said she didn't know if her daughter had allergies, only that she did suffer fits as a child and often had convulsions. Asked if she had ever been treated for them, Elisabeth was forced to say no. Dr Reiter asked her how many times Kerstin had been treated by a doctor for any condition over the years and Elisabeth was forced to admit that her daughter had never set foot in a surgery. This was at odds with the caring note that Fritzl had produced with a flourish and also jarred with what Dr Reiter could sense was an underlying sense of real and heartfelt love that the woman obviously had for her daughter.

'Will she be all right, doctor?' she asked.

Dr Reiter could give no guarantees about the recovery

prospects for the young woman who was hooked up to a bewildering assortment of machines and instruments. Fritzl and Elisabeth left the hospital. They had only gone a few yards when two men in dark suits appeared, flashing the credentials of police detectives.

'We would like to have a few words with you at the station,' one said.

Herr Polzer recalls: 'There was no struggle, no attempts at resisting. Had there been, they would both have been arrested.'

And Fritzl thought it had all gone so well.

At Amstetten police station Elisabeth was taken to one room, her father to another.

The police said they had received a call from the hospital that evening to report 'suspicious individuals' visiting Kerstin. 'Where have you been, Frau Fritzl?' they asked Elisabeth.

But she was terrified; her children were still in that house and her tormentor still held enormous sway over her. The clock in the interview room showed it was close to 10.00 p.m. and she had never been apart from Felix and Stefan since they were born. A flurry of confused and painful thoughts flooded through her; she wanted to end the misery they endured but she was frightened out of her wits.

Herr Polzer describes the tension in the interview room: 'She was told that if she didn't talk about matters, she would lay herself open to charges of the most serious kind of child abandonment – carrying the most serious penalties.'

But Elisabeth's moment had come. She had tasted freedom and she liked its flavour. She had long ago thought herself dead, conditioned herself to think she would never leave the catacomb. Now she had a new chance at life – but she had to gain one vital, soul-preserving concession if she was to tell these policemen the story they would never forget, that they might well not believe.

She looked up, brushing back the white hair from her pinched and sallow face and said: 'I have a lot to tell you, but can you promise me one thing? Will you promise me that I will never, ever see him again? This story is not what you think it is. I can tell you another story.'

The officers said they could make that guarantee if that was her wish. But they also reminded her that she was suspected of abuse and cruelty towards her children, and they could make no deals if she incriminated herself.

She made a curious half-smile to herself, sipped from a proffered glass of water and spoke. 'I was kidnapped by my father when I was 18 and have been raped by him for 24 years. He first began to abuse me when I was 11. Kerstin is his daughter. I have had six other children by him, one of whom died in his cellar. I have never seen other human beings for 24 years before this day, except him and my children.' And she led them on a guided tour of the depravity of the man: the rapes in front of her children; the baby he burned; the terror he instilled; the lives he stole. 'I don't know why, but my father chose me for himself,' she added. Two hours later, at 12.15 a.m., the Amstetten police protocol records show that the interview was concluded. Two notebooks had been filled, two cassette recordings made. Elisabeth had taken 124 minutes to describe her life underground.

The police officers were shocked – speechless – it had

all come out without prompting, delivered in the tones of someone who seemed unused to talking, unsure of words. They didn't want to believe it. Could the man who sat in an interview room a few feet away from them have been so evil? Far easier to believe this woman was simply trying to wriggle out of a charge of neglect.

But the more they looked at the facts, the more they made sense. The three unregistered children, and the physical condition of them all – from the pale skin to the missing teeth.

One of the officers who was in the interview room that night says: 'It was like a bomb had gone off. We knew we'd be working now on the most important case of our lives, that everything that had gone before and everything that would come after would fade into insignificance at the monumental scale of what had taken place at Ybbsstrasse. It didn't seem possible that this ragged, bedraggled woman could have survived that hell. She slumped at the end, exhausted from it all. Words of comfort just seemed too trite and out of place. What could any of us possibly do to alleviate the suffering of this poor, poor woman? Inadequate is too small a word to describe how we all felt. But we knew that we would hold good to our word and, if she chose, she would never have to see Josef Fritzl again.'

Polzer recalls: 'I got the call at 2.00 a.m. on Sunday morning about what had happened, and I was there three hours later. Elisabeth had related her 24 years in that hell in just about two hours. The way she said it, the other facts taken into consideration . . . I can only say that it all seemed to be true.'

Fritzl, in an adjoining room, was saying nothing. If anything, he expected to be told that his daughter was to be charged with endangering her children. Apparently he was 'friendly, but monosyllabic'. An officer said later: 'He was agitated that his daughter wasn't with him. He kept glancing nervously at the door. He was clearly becoming aware that in the past he had always controlled doors, controlled her. Now he had lost control.'

Fritzl glanced up as the door was opened by the detectives who had been interviewing Elisabeth. He smiled his glib smile. It was still on his face as the handcuffs snapped on his wrists.

It was over.

Ybbsstrasse 40, Amstetten, 8.00 a.m., Sunday 27 April, 2008

As head of the criminal division of the local police Leopold Etz could have been forgiven for thinking he had seen it all in his years as an officer. When he went to open the cellar door at Ybbsstrasse 40, it must have felt comparable to the moment when the famous Egyptologist Howard Carter opened the tomb of the boy pharaoh Tutankhamun in 1922. The big difference of course is that Carter famously said 'wonderful things', when asked what he could see when the seal to the tomb was broken after 3,000 years.

For Etz, there was nothing wonderful to behold at the bottom of the 11 steps that led to the underground empire of Josef Fritzl as the gatekeeper punched in the key code which revealed the hidden cellar. What Etz saw will haunt him for the rest of his days. Like policemen everywhere, he thought he was inured to the suffering of humans: the shot, the stabbed, the randomly abused, the raped, the drugged, the desperate. Yet there is no parallel to the crime which was laid bare in the split seconds after the concrete door to the cellar slid back, nothing with which to compare it. The strip lighting within went on and the vision of Fritzl's unique brand of hell was revealed.

Etz and the other officers gagged on the stench from the toilet, and recoiled from the mould growing on the walls of the dungeon where seven children had been born, and three had been raised. And then there was the filthy shower curtain, the water dripping from the ceiling. They stared, unable to speak. Hard-cop banter and glib phrases dried up. 'Jesus Christ,' said one. 'I thought the concentration camps ended years ago.' Fritzl was led away to a police car, his final task accomplished.

'We needed him there to get us through all the locked doors,' explains Polzer. 'He kept the old TV remote control in a drawer in the room before the last door. That last door was hidden, not by a sliding cupboard but by one that had to be dismantled and reassembled every time he went in there. He had his work cut out for him all right.'

Hours earlier, before Fritzl took him downstairs to tour his lair, Etz had been to the Fritzl residence to find the former dwellers of this revolting, inhumane bunker resting upstairs with their grandmother.

'It was the boys, Stefan and Felix,' he recalls, sitting with Rosemarie when the officers entered in the small hours of the morning. They both looked terrified and were terribly pale. They were led out to waiting cars while officers tried to explain the unimaginable to Rosemarie. 'This was the first time they had been out in the real world in their lives,' says Etz, recounting how he led them down from the Fritzl flat to an Amstetten street that would never be the same again.

The boys walked a little like drunken sailors; they had moved for so long like dwarf miners in a wretched Grimm gallery that they had trouble coordinating their movements, felt giddy and disorientated. Then, when Felix was led outside for the first time in his life and he looked up at the sky, he pointed and said: 'Is that where God lives?' Hardened police officers found it hard to keep the tears at bay when they heard that.

'Everything was new and it was clear they were amazed. The only idea they had of the real world was what they'd seen on television,' adds Etz. In the dark, the boys entered cars for the first time in their lives, and were told they were off to rejoin their mother. 'It was their first car ride ever,' continues Etz, 'and they were amazed at the speed and really excited. They'd never known anything like it. They'd only ever seen cars on the TV. Travelling in one was a totally different experience, especially for Felix who was beside himself with excitement. He was shrieking with pleasure when he saw cars coming the other way, and he and his brother braced themselves whenever a car went past. They thought there was going to be a head-on crash. They were fascinated by the headlights. They were shouting and hiding behind the seats. The best bit, though, was when they saw the moon. They were just open-mouthed with awe, and were nudging each other and pointing. They'd never even seen the moon.'

The boys were to be reunited with their mother. Meanwhile, the policemen would be returning to the dungeon – to probe its secrets and learn of its silent, brooding capacity to instil docility in the residents forced to live within it.

'In all my years as a policeman I've seen a lot, but I've never seen anything like this,' says Etz. The chamber was a horror to the police officers assigned to search it – and they never even had to spend a day or night in it. Nor could they; the air was so foul that 11 criminologists working in shifts rotated every two hours before coming up for fresh air. Within a week a new ventilation system pumping cold, fresh air was installed to allow the experts to work longer underground.

The pictures of the cellar shocked the world. As well as the appallingly cramped and fetid conditions, there were the human touches that testified to the spirit of those forced to live there. Felix had drawn and pasted a blue octopus on to the wall of the shower; Kerstin drew pictures of fruit that grew on trees she had never seen. These were pathetic links to 'the outside' they were told was not for them, drawn from images seen flickering on the colour TV set.

An impression of how vile the place was can be gauged by the fact that the police tasked to probe it were themselves ordered to undergo psychological counselling as they felt crushed by its claustrophobic feel and 'unutterable sadness' at the pitiful drawings the cave children had made on the walls. 'What the officers had to look at down there was terrible,' says Polzer. 'Going into the cellar was like climbing into an old submarine.' The shower curtain was covered in mould and he described the toilet – which was in the kitchen, where all their food was prepared – as being in a 'catastrophic state', not for want of attempted cleanliness, but because the sanitation was simply inadequate for the needs of four inhabitants plus, when he was around, Fritzl the jailer.

'The stench was, truly, almost unbearable,' asserts Polzer. 'It was, without doubt, the most inhumane crime scene I have ever encountered. OK, it wasn't a complex case, because he was to admit it and all the evidence was there. But on a human level . . . every glass, every picture on every wall, every artefact was touched by humans forced to live there for years on end. It was horrifying; it is horrifying. To think that Elisabeth survived the first years there alone, without anyone but her father coming down to violate her. Then she's raped by him and bears his children, completely alone without any help from him.

'Then she summons up the strength and courage to nourish these children, to teach them to walk, to read, to write and to do multiplication. She can't teach them to jump because there's no room to jump down there.

'She cooked for them and washed for them and loved them. From the moment of their birth until the day they were freed there was not one second, not one second, when she wasn't with them. There were no kindergarten breaks for her, no time off. She was an incredible mother to them under incredible circumstances.'

Polzer, a man not given to hyperbole or exaggeration, said as the aftershocks of the earthquake rumbled through

Austria and beyond: 'The description she gave was beyond the belief of the police officers. He pressured her physically to keep her there and sexually abused this young woman, his own daughter, over many years. The result of his criminal activities has been to break this woman. This case knows no precedents or comparisons in Austrian history.'

Polzer came under pressure from conspiracy theorists and an insatiable media to point the finger at others. Surely Fritzl had accomplices; surely Rosemarie must have known what was taking place beneath the foundations of Ybbsstrasse; surely he abused other children in the family. The answers were no, no and – maybe. At the time of writing the police have had no opportunity to get close to the upstairs clan or the downstairs dwellers. It is unclear what Elisabeth has told them. Often in incest families, abusers will target more than one vulnerable victim. But, as events have shown, Fritzl was no ordinary abuser and this was no ordinary case.

Polzer has confirmed the premeditation with which Fritzl planned and built his bunker: 'We are working with certainty on the idea that already in the planning phase he had the intention to build a small space, a small secret . . . a small dungeon unknown to the building authorities.'

Polzer's investigators have established that Fritzl installed eight doors in the warren-like complex that separated Elisabeth and her children from the outside world. Five of the doors were opened with a 'highly sophisticated' cylinder key; the others were electronically operated via a key-code device. 'We're not talking here of a Harry Potter film in which you press against a secret door and it opens,' adds Polzer. He explains that part of the cellar consists of rooms built in the late 19th century under the existing family house which Fritzl began extending in 1979, having received planning permission. He also adds: 'It does seem that he wanted to free himself from his responsibilities and return his victims to some sort of normal life.' Polzer speculates that the timetable for this liberation was set roughly for the summer of 2008.

Inevitably and speedily, the Fritzl case drew parallels with that of Natascha Kampusch, and it was only a matter of hours before the survivor of that particular ordeal appeared on TV offering her sympathy to the family. Bizarrely, Miss Kampusch suggested that Elisabeth and her children should have been left where they were, adding: 'I believe it might have been better to leave them where they were – although that was probably impossible – because that was, of course, their environment. Pulling them abruptly out of there without any transition and isolating them cannot be good for them.' Ultimately, however, Ms Kampusch came across to many as a survivor who seemed to want to reflect the dramatic moment of their freedom back on herself. 'Little by little I realized there were parallels to my own fate,' she added, 'so then the whole story affected me even more.' She went on to say that the experts who were dealing with them were 'probably wrong' – which perhaps says much about the therapy she has received and what good she thinks it did her.

In a second later interview with the BBC she picked up on the theme of the Nazis having been a major factor in shaping Fritzl's criminal mind. 'At the time of National

Socialism the suppression of women was propagated. An authoritarian education was very important,' she said. Fritzl would admit as much less than a month later. Order, discipline, obedience – the trinity had failed him. Instead, the love of the illicit clan would prove stronger than Fritzl's perverted master plan.

As for Amstetten, local mayor Helmut Katzengruber struggles to find some sense of perspective as the shock-waves of the earthquake reverberate through the community. He was drinking the local fermented pear juice, when: 'I got a call from the director of the city utilities, he had been contacted by journalists. It was all so unbelievable, something you couldn't take in. It was on Sunday, 27 April, midday, that I heard, and by then the family were already in the clinic, all of them except Kerstin, who was at the hospital.

'It was so unbelievable that I didn't want to, couldn't believe it . . . Before the call I'd been celebrating the first of that year's bottles of liqueur. After that the world changed. Of course we cancelled the festival. We've spent 40 years building up the Amstetten reputation for a producer of this drink. Now all the world knows us for something completely different and all because of one man.'

One man who is likely to remain Amstetten's most famous son.

9. Secrets and Lies Revealed

The land without maps lies in the Regional Clinic Most-viertel in Mauer. It is a place of refuge for Elisabeth, the cellar children, the upstairs family and Rosemarie. The clinic resembles a fortress rather than a hospital: armed police outside, security staff inside, CCTV cameras monitoring every inch of ground to keep the world's press at bay from a family trying to recover from the unimaginable.

The clinic is a leading centre for psychiatric care, reputedly one of the finest in Europe. But just as Nazism shaped the character of Josef Fritzl, helped him to formulate his elaborate crime, so the clinic has its dark secrets too. Order, discipline, obedience translated into cruel deaths here during the Third Reich. The ghosts of SS killers stalk the very rooms where the family take the first faltering steps towards recovery. The clinic was formerly a euthanasia centre where the 'useless eaters' of the state – the mentally and physically handicapped, the genetically disordered, the half- and often simply the slow-witted – were murdered here by the same good Austrians who would go on to excel in the wholesale extermination of the Jews during the Second World War.

'The first step to eliminating inherited and mental diseases was sterilization,' records a book commissioned by the town chronicling the Nazi period. At least 346 people were killed with lethal injections in the clinic in 'the last step – euthanasia'. Patients were also sent to Gugging, near Vienna, where Dr Emil Gelny gained notoriety for his killings. Gelny visited the Mauer clinic in 1944 to kill what he deemed 'unnecessary mouths'. He killed at least 39 people with drugs such as veronal, luminal and morphine. Gelny fled Vienna at the end of the war, moving first to Syria and then Baghdad, where he died in peace as a reputable doctor in 1961, his victims unavenged.

There are no Gelnys any more at the clinic. If there were, they would surely have deemed the wretches from the subterranean warren fit for his disposal methods. Elisabeth, aged way beyond her years, partially toothless, suffering chronic vitamin deficiencies and internal scarring from unattended childbirth and unwanted sexual mistreatment. The boys Stefan and Felix, their muscles wasted, their joints stiff, their bones malformed through the long years of living in a dungeon. At the beginning they suffered particularly badly from vitamin D deficiency and were put on a rigorous exercise programme. All had sallow skin, various forms of gum disease, retinal damage, and chronically weakened immune systems.

This is what is visible. Unlocking the secrets of their tortured minds is much more difficult and requires therapy of a far more complex nature that will stretch down the years, possibly well into old age, and costing many hundreds of thousands of euros. They will have to learn to live with themselves, to try to understand and overcome the effects of the lifelong abuse they endured.

They also have to overcome the corrosive effects of

hatred. Elisabeth in particular hates her father for what he did to her, but the doctors tell her that, just as alcoholics and drug addicts in the 12-step programme are told to have animosities towards no one, she has to let go, to forgive while never forgetting. They say it will be better for her in the long run.

Although she and the children have experienced the joy of relief and release, and the simple, sensual pleasures of such things as fresh air and sunlight, a blue sky and an open door, they have suffered mental wounds as traumatic as those of soldiers under shellfire. Like survivors of war, the post-traumatic stress syndrome will spook and stalk them long into the future. Perhaps, believe the doctors, only little Felix may be young enough to escape the demons.

He has reduced staff at the hospital to tears with his wonderment at the world. He needs no PlayStation, Nintendo or Atari gizmos to bring joy to his innocent face; a ride in a car and a glimpse of thunder clouds bedazzle him. He may, hope the doctors, be young enough even to erase most of the memories of his early years in the cellar. But things are being taken at the speed of drying paint.

Life in the cellar was slow time, like that experienced by prisoners everywhere: life in molasses. By necessity, to deal with the shock, disorientation, anger, guilt and sadness – as well as the positive emotions felt after release – the healing process is also excruciatingly slow. Elisabeth is being coached to gradually express her own needs and feelings. Life skills ebbed away in the cellar. What does she know of using a telephone, shopping, making small talk, asking for something when everything was always provided? The most delicate aspect of her therapy involves not asking too many questions of her too quickly. Just as soldiers who experienced horrific scenes in the front line of battle are not asked to recount them, so the carers have been told by the chief psychiatrist charged with trying to restore a semblance of normality to her and the children not to probe into Elisabeth's feelings too deeply or too swiftly. Treading heavily into the areas still mined with pain could make her feel she is being abused all over again, and lead to flashbacks which will land her right back in that grim subterranean grotto.

Another huge task is restoring the 'R' word to Elisabeth and the children: respect. Astonishing as it may sound to those whose only experience of such nightmares has been through the prism of the TV lens or the newspaper headline, victims like Elisabeth often carry with them, buried deep, the notion that they were somehow responsible for what occurred to them. Her father stripped away all her self-esteem and for 24 years she was shown no respect. 'She may expect punishment or blame in equal measure,' commented one expert. 'She may even have quite hysterical fears of abuse from her carers.' She will have to look to her therapists for everything; to tell her what to do at all times. She was the strong mother of the cellar; in the clinic, she is the teenager whose clock stopped all those years ago. Very gradually, with infinite patience and care, it is slowly being rewound to start anew.

Victims of sexual abuse commonly express feelings of extreme guilt: guilt that they didn't, or couldn't, stop the abuse, guilt that they 'let' it go on for so long, guilt that the abuser has been arrested. Natascha Kampusch, another survivor of underground imprisonment and abuse, is the only similar study experts can refer to. Kidnapped at the age of ten in 1998, she emerged from an eight-and-a-half-year incarceration at the hands of her predator, Wolfgang Priklopil, in 2006.

Ms Kampusch has been extremely secretive about the facts of her captivity, perhaps as a way of coping with it. She has never spoken of her true feelings for her captor, but they were, and remain, deeply complex. In the spring of this year an Austrian newspaper published the police interviews with her in which she admitted consensual sex with him: she still carries around a picture of him in her handbag; she wept over his coffin when he committed suicide in the hours following her escape, accusing the police of 'murdering' him. And in May of 2008 she purchased his 'House of Horrors' from his elderly mother, with its cellar lair still intact, in what she said was a move designed to prevent it being vandalized or purchased by a developer to bulldoze for a new housing estate.

In many ways Natascha Kampusch remains a captive of the cellar, and it is that bond with the past that the carers of Elisabeth must break if she is to stand a chance of forging an existence of meaning and quality in the years that remain ahead of her. Part of the therapy programme involves her reciting short mantras to herself. They include: 'It was not my fault, I did the best I could'; 'He was the bad one'; 'He cannot hurt me any more'; 'I am OK'; 'Those who truly love me care about what I want, what I think, and what I feel'.

The Stockholm Syndrome – describing the emotional attachment that forms between captives and captors – has been identified in at least some of the children, both the above-ground tribe and the cellar brood, but none in Elisabeth. The victims in circumstances such as the captivity endured by Elisabeth and her children may vehemently defend the perpetrator and even apportion much of the blame to themselves, particularly where they have been told by the abuser that they are to blame. The hatred that she professes for her father saves Elisabeth from this, but she must wrestle with what she will tell her children when they ask: 'Why us, Mummy? Why didn't you get him to let us out earlier? Why didn't you treat him better, and give us the chance of freedom sooner?' Nothing Elisabeth could have done would have given the secret family their freedom sooner than it came; but the doubts and questions of scarred children have to be addressed.

Another 'R' word useful in the healing process is: routine. Elisabeth established her own timetable for her children but, in actuality, all life below ground was dictated by Fritzl the jailer. Elisabeth is being taught to be the mistress of her own time – how to manage it, fill it, appreciate it.

Elisabeth, who is getting to know her mother after all the lost years, met with Rosemarie daily on an adjoining ward during the first month of freedom. They made breakfasts of rolls, coffee, cereal, fruit, ham and cheese while the children made their beds. Routine gave purpose to a life where the spirit had been sapped by the cruelty of her incarceration, a place where she truly thought she would die, and it brings purpose back to a life on the outside she hopes soon to rejoin.

At 42, Elisabeth is still of an age to find a partner to care for her and share her life with. Her psychiatric care is ongoing. She has been prescribed a course of psychotropic medications to provide relief from intrusive symptoms of fear, anxiety and low self-esteem. Even though her prolonged incarceration and abuse are without parallel, certainly in modern times, she is not alone. There are other survivors out there.

The physical pace of life is markedly different for the family who lived upstairs, went to school and enjoyed sunlight and seasons, as compared to the below-stairs clan. Elisabeth and the cellar children tire much more quickly than the others. Elisabeth even needs to take a nap every afternoon because she is exhausted, whereas her much older mother can go through the day until lights out at 10.00 p.m. without a rest.

The meeting between Elisabeth's upstairs and below-stairs children occurred even before DNA tests had confirmed that they were all Josef Fritzl's incestuous offspring. Stefan and Felix, still scared of strangers and the sunshine, were greeted warmly by the two teenage girls from upstairs, Monika, 15, and Lisa, 14, and their 11-year-old brother, Alexander. 'It was a genuinely happy occasion, not forced, as was the very moving meeting between Rosemarie and Elisabeth,' recalls their chief doctor, Berthold Kepplinger. 'We are looking after all of them with a large team of child and adult psychologists, therapists, neurologists, logopedists and physiotherapists.

Each of the patients is traumatized in a different way and we are giving them individual therapy.'

Their mental scars are all different, as illustrated by a further comment from Dr Kepplinger. He says the boys viewed Fritzl 'differently' from the females of the family. With no significant other male figure in the lives of the upstairs children – and none at all for the downstairs clan, save Fritzl – it is feared the boys have an ingrained sense of respect for him, perhaps even believing that Fritzl wasn't so bad after all. This misplaced admiration is being addressed as a matter of some urgency if they are to stand a chance of recovery.

Amid the therapy sessions there have also been visitors. Elisabeth's sister Gabriele Helm, 36, admitted she broke down and wept when she first met her after she was freed. Elisabeth vanished when she was 18, and Gabriele bought into the fiction of her joining a cult like everyone else. And, like everyone else in that dominated and abused family, she was permanently in the thrall of a father she respected and feared. Gabriele, who is herself undergoing therapy, says: 'None of us can believe how normal Elisabeth seems. She's healthy and very chatty and doing very well. Every day she gets a bit stronger. I can't say what the family is going through. It's more than anyone can believe. It has devastated us. We are working together to support Elisabeth. She is overjoyed to see her children. She told them they were beautiful, stroked their faces one by one, and told them how precious they were to her.'

Elisabeth and Felix have to wear special polarizing glasses because their eyes are so sensitive to natural light. They laugh and joke, miming bespectacled characters on

the DVDs and videos that play on the TV, just as it once
played in their cellar, the transmitter from a distant star
that brought relief, but no hope of escape. The hospital
television is only equipped to play recorded films; the
family are deliberately being quarantined from the stories
running about them in the media. In the hospital, the TV
is rarely off, offering as it does glimpses of a world waiting
to be rediscovered. They watch nature documentaries,
children's cartoons and travel programmes, the latter
offering truly amazing scenes for children whose previous
frontiers extended to just yards in front of their faces.
Three weeks into their stay at the clinic, Elisabeth had
her first taste of the outside world. With the paparazzi
laying siege to the clinic, in the hope of the million-dollar
snapshot of the 'cellar mother' or her brood, she resorted
to donning a nurse's uniform for her first walk outside.

The excursion into this alien environment was sanc-
tioned by Dr Kepplinger. He ordered plain-clothes detectives dressed as orderlies and patients to stay close to her
at all times and stipulated she should spend no more than
15 minutes outside.

Elisabeth was led down a back staircase in a uniform,
black lace-up flat shoes, black tights, a wig and a blue
cardigan. Onlookers thought she appeared frail but
excited, her eyes were lit up. Female employees cried
when they saw her. She was with a carer at all times and
put her arm through hers as she moved about the
grounds. Once she stopped to pluck a pink rhododendron
flower that was just coming into bloom and took it back
to the ward with her, twirling it in her hands. She has the
status of a hero in the hospital.

On several other occasions Elisabeth was allowed out to see her comatose daughter Kerstin, being cared for in the Amstetten hospital several kilometres away. 'Elisabeth is guarded like the crown jewels,' a male nurse told the *Österreich* newspaper. 'When she went out she was also disguised as a nurse on these occasions and even put on a red wig with a ponytail.' Elisabeth sat quietly at the edge of the bed as her daughter's weakened immune system struggled to overcome the paralyzing effects of her long imprisonment. Other times she spoke with her. Later, after doctors brought Kerstin out of her artificially induced coma, they would say the love that radiated from Elisabeth was instrumental, vital even, in bringing her daughter back to the land of the living.

Her lawyer, Christoph Herbst, has described those first few weeks of freedom: 'Elisabeth is very happy to be re-discovering the world. She is very keen to go outside and feel the rain on her skin. But it is important for them to adjust slowly. For the most part they just talk to each other. Elisabeth and her children who lived in the cellar have little concept of time and of the future. Some people who hear the story think Elisabeth is like something from a horror film. But rumours that she has no teeth and can't talk are not true. She lost a lot of teeth, but not all of them. If you met her you wouldn't realize what she's been through, as she seems just like every normal person. She tells her family that all she longs for is a normal life – or as normal a life as they can get. That's her only wish.

'They just, very much, need peace; they have to relax. They have to get together right now – the part of the family who lived with the grandmother, the part of the family who lived with the mother. So they're getting further treatment by therapists. I'd say in the next weeks they just have to get used to a more normal life. And they feel, I'd say, pretty much comfortable in their new environment, although it's not the sort of environment in which they'll most likely live in the future. They don't have access to the media. They don't have a television set. They don't have a radio. They don't have newspapers, for good reasons, because I think if they really understood what's going on in the media, they'd be completely . . . let's put it this way, they wouldn't really understand the world and right now they really need time for themselves.

'The family lives together – the grandmother, Elisabeth and their children. They have, let's say, a more or less regular life now. They get up, some earlier than the others. That's normal in such a big family. They rise at about six to seven in the morning. Then they have breakfast together. They get their breakfast from the hospital. Then they sit together at a large table and talk, discuss and make jokes. Then everybody does their own thing; they play on the computer; they read books; do some drawings; everybody does whatever they want to do. Sometimes the children go to their own room, do their own things. Sometimes they play with toys. They have an aquarium and all those things. Then they have lunch, and after lunch, if they want, they take a nap, then again the same procedure. Right now the older children will have school lessons so that they have more or less their normal life and challenges, so it's not as if they don't have any-thing to do. And then it's dinner time, and then they have time to watch videos or listen to music. And then it's time for bed.

'It's very amazing to watch the family because they behave like a normal family, and if you meet them, you're kind of part of the family. You have to play with them, to chat with them, to discuss things with them, and therefore you feel better than you did before.

'They are on one floor in this building, in the hospital, and there are several rooms. And then there's one central room where they can meet, have their breakfast, lunch and dinner. But they have, kind of, the atmosphere of an apartment – and, if they want, they can go into their rooms, where they can sleep or where they can do their own things. They have kind of a feeling, as if it was a sort of an apartment, a kind of home, but of course it's not similar to what we experience in our life . . . the children share bedrooms; the sisters sleep together; the brothers sleep together and Elisabeth with the little one.

'Elisabeth: she's a normal-looking woman. It's a normal family with a very strong woman – that's important to understand. Felix is a very smart young boy. He's very bright, he makes jokes, he surprises the family as any small child often surprises their family. He causes laughter and smiles for the whole group so he is doing really well. He gets more vivid from day to day. He loves to be loved by everybody so he understands that he's the one who makes everybody happy . . . Stefan, who is the older one, is a little bit more than 18 years old. He is more the quiet one who tries to take care of everyone and takes over the role as the eldest one.

'As regards the children who lived with the grand-mother, things are completely different because right now they can't go out. They don't have the freedom they had before. So for them this is very difficult to understand; they can't go out because journalists are waiting in front of the hospital in order to take photographs . . . They can't see their friends, they can't meet their classmates, they even miss school, and this is something that is very hard for them. We all hope this situation will change soon because they have to have their normal life again.

'It's completely true that life has changed enormously for Stefan and for Felix, but I think they're still missing lots of things they would like to experience in the outside world. For instance, some days ago it rained and Felix just said "I want to see rain for the first time" because "I never saw that" and, if you hear that, you just realize yes, he hasn't ever seen that before. He said the other day there was a thunderstorm and for the first time he experienced its noise, and it was a sense of wonderment for him.

'Something which is really amazing is that Elisabeth gets along very well with the three children who lived with the grandmother and, as far as I heard from the doctors, this was from the first day onwards. And also the kids really welcomed their mother very, very warmly. They really got along very well from the first time. They enjoy their mother. It's a little bit of a funny situation for them but they're happy to be together.

'Elisabeth feels well if the children feel well; she gets her strength from them. She thinks and feels for the whole family. She understands whatever we speak about.

She decides rather quickly. She knows what she wants. So I think, as I said before, really she is a very impressive and very strong woman.

'I think there's no indication what the future will bring or how long they must remain in the hospital. The first indications of how long they must remain will only come after two to three months, but definitely not earlier than that. We have had discussions about whether we want to proceed against Josef Fritzl for damages. This is something that has to be discussed beforehand with Elisabeth. But this is something that has not yet been decided. Then there is the criminal case, which has not yet started. We'll have to see what happens. The point is, this is a decision that has to be taken by Elisabeth if she wants compensation for the damages that have been caused by her father.

'As to the long-term future, they have to decide together with the doctors and the therapists where they will live and who will live with whom. Again, this is not something that is completely clear, nor is the issue yet settled as to whether they will change identities. These are things that cannot be addressed right now.'

In the second week of June, 2008, the hospital relocated the family from the ward to an apartment – usually used as an official residence for visiting doctors – where they could all be together. The fact that the Fritzl clan has taken up residence in the apartment shows how long-term their therapy must be. Ten days after Kerstin was woken from her artificial coma on June 1, 2008, a furniture company's delivery truck was spotted unloading nine single beds, wardrobes, a settee and a side table, curtains, lamps, a TV set, a fridge, a microwave, a clothes horse, garden furniture and toys at the clinic.

These are the building blocks of a return to a normality the cellar children never knew. The psychological impact on the upstairs family of finding out that their grandfather is also their father still has to be assessed. While life is difficult for them because of the sedentary pace of the therapy programme, doctors want them there because they say it is vital for the mother–children bond to be established as quickly as possible, for the youngsters who lived above to know that they always had a real mother below ground who loved them every bit as much as their grandmother, Rosemarie.

But they have built up resentments at being confined in the way their unknown siblings were confined, isolated from the friends they know, the schools they attended. As Christoph Herbst has explained, they long for a speedy return to their old life, but this may never be possible. The world's press is destined to pursue this family to the ends of the earth – or to the end of their lives, if necessary.

New identities and a new start somewhere far away from Amstetten, possibly far away from Austria, are being mooted by those who are now caring for Elisabeth and her family. The Austrian state, smarting from international criticism about how the affair was allowed to go on for as long as it did, will accede to any wish that the family or their carers deem appropriate. But already there are those who say the same mistakes are being made with Elisabeth as were made with Natascha Kampusch.

Elisabeth's former school friend Christa Woldrich says:

'They wouldn't let me see her, which I could accept if it came from Elisabeth, but they're just making these decisions on their own. I've spoken to her lawyer, Dr Herbst, but he's not interested in helping me. I told him I believe Elisabeth needs her friends around her. Instead, she's surrounded again by lawyers and medics – just like Natascha. I'm sure if she were asked she would want to see some of us.' Christa has now released a CD to help raise cash for her former pal and her family; it's being sold around Amstetten and she's sent a copy to the hospital where Elisabeth is living. 'I've been having nightmares, thinking about what happened to her all that time, and I wanted to do something more to help. If I can't see her – at least I can do my bit in other ways.'

For the outside world the information about how they are coping remains scant. But there was a message from within the clinic walls delivered to the people of Amstetten and those further afield on 15 May, 2008. It took the form of brightly coloured handprints, hearts, smiley faces and rainbows with little bits of text, thanking a world that cared for the children who thought they'd been forgotten. Two of the three cellar children drew the images – Kerstin was still in her coma at the time – as well as Elisabeth, Rosemarie and the upstairs children. The text read:

We, the whole family, would like to use this opportunity to thank you all for sympathizing with our fate. Your empathy is helping us to go through these difficult times and it shows us that there also are good and honest people. We hope that there will be a time when we can return to normal life.

The poster was pinned up in a shop in the centre of Amstetten. In a text written within an open pair of hands, Elisabeth wrote:

> *I wish for: the recovery of my daughter Kerstin, the love of my children, the protection of my family, for people with a big heart and compassion.*

In a personal note resembling that of his siblings and his mother, Stefan wrote:

> *I miss my sister. I am happy about my freedom and about my family. I like the sun, the fresh air and nature.*

His writing was spidery but it proved one thing – Elisabeth had struggled in their dungeon hell to ensure the cave children did not grow up to be cavemen. Grandmother Rosemarie wrote a note signed only as 'grandma' that read:

> *I wish to be able to live in peace with my children, with much strength and with God's help. I miss my dear friends and my freedom.*

Felix, the youngest sibling, wrote in his personal note that he dreamed of playing with other children and running in the meadows, as well as of riding in cars and on sledges.

Lawyer Herbst comments: 'As you may know, a poster was disclosed to the public and this idea to produce such a poster was initiated by the family itself, in particular by the children. They just wanted to express themselves;

they just wanted to have some contact with the outside world; they wanted to say thank you for the support they'd heard that the public would give them, and I think it was also some fun for the kids because they loved to do it. Felix in particular was very happy that his hands were part of this poster.

'It's true that Elisabeth tried to educate the children in the dungeon. They had lessons; they learned grammar; they learned the language, mathematics. So they've been raised very well; they're very well behaved. It's really astounding if you experience Stefan. He is a very polite and educated person, and so I think Elisabeth tried her best to give them a structure and a good life under the given circumstances in the dungeon.'

Dr Kepplinger has confirmed: 'The family circumstances are good and improving. The therapy team aims to provide the family with help for a new start, for a new life in the future. It's therefore necessary to slowly and carefully adapt the family to reality.'

His team includes speech therapists. Although it is true that little Felix and Stefan did like to grunt and growl in a kind of made-up language, the initial press reports that they were something straight out of Rudyard Kipling's *Jungle Book* have been dismissed by Dr Kepplinger. 'Most of the speech they heard came from a television that was on in the cellar most of the time. They communicate with each other, but in a far from normal way.' Their mother taught them some reading and writing, although Elisabeth herself lost much of her childhood knowledge due to the years of abuse that began when she was 11 and her imprisonment from the age of 18. There were few books in the dungeon, save for the ones on childbirth that Fritzl bought for Elisabeth when she was about to go into labour. Fritzl did buy some children's books years later, but the main source of education, over the years, was the television.

'Both suffer from vitamin D deficiency resulting from lack of sunlight, but that should be cured given time,' adds Dr Kepplinger. 'The mother and the smallest child have, in just the last couple of days, increased their sensitivity to light, so they have protective sunglasses. Felix is getting more and more lively. He's fascinated by everything that he sees around him – the fresh air, the light, and the food – all of these things are helping them. Slowly the colour of all their skins is changing back to a more normal shade.

'The family members have been brought things they were used to, such as an aquarium and toys for the children. Stefan had a fish tank in the cellar and he missed having one here. The family is finding each other again and those who didn't know each other are getting to know each other. The family are having very lively conversations.

'Time must have passed very slowly in the dungeon. This slow-moving time is something we want to maintain in the clinic. Our policy all along has been to avoid too much therapy. Every one of them has unique problems that need to be addressed in different ways, but we need to take it slowly. The children who lived upstairs are used to a different speed of life, and we've offered them more to do. The young people have space to play, they can run around. They enjoy the food especially, and on April 29th the family held an impromptu birthday party with a cake for the second-youngest, 12-year-old Alexander. He also got stuffed animals and Lego as presents. Elisabeth is coping very well, considering everything, but what occurred was definitely dreadful for her and for her children.

'A completely new family is slowly coming into existence here. The boys are making a good recovery, especially Felix. Both are polite and seem to have had respect instilled into them. They do exactly what their mother tells them. Felix has a keen intelligence which shows with his enthusiasm for everything. We love his wit and outgoing personality.'

Felix is learning to forget. But Fritzl, his father, grandfather, gatekeeper, soul-crusher and life-stealer, will never have that luxury. He thinks about his cellar family constantly, or so he says – and, given his 24-year vocation to discipline them, earn their obedience and instil order, there is no reason to disbelieve him. His massive libido is diminished but it will never leave him. The world's opprobrium – aside from his cellmate – is his only companion. Prison is a lonely place for Josef Fritzl, forever condemned to be known as 'The Beast of Amstetten'. He is now experiencing what it is like to have his freedom restricted by others. He used to dictate the pace of life for his secret family; now jailers dictate it for him.

He has read some of the letters that flooded into the jail following his arrest, but not all of them. He doesn't need to read any more to get the picture of what the outside world thinks of him; he doesn't need a hearing aid to listen to what his fellow inmates think of him. 'Satan,' they yell through the bars of their cell doors. 'You bastard'; 'pervert'; 'kid-f***er': these are some of the more polite epithets.

There is a darker side to human nature. People like Fritzl are a magnet to lonely women, many of whom think he is misunderstood and should be forgiven. Among the mail he has received in his prison cell were, by mid-June, some letters proposing marriage, support, offering prayers and affection. It is unclear what, if any, succour he takes from these missives that mirror the letters sent by women to death-row inmates in America.

He chooses not to take his exercise breaks; he eats his breakfast of tea and black bread, lunch of cutlet and noodles or chopped steak and potatoes, and evening meal of sausages, ham and cheese, in his cell. In the way of prisons all over the world, sex offenders are somewhere below cockroaches in the esteem of convicts. By reason of the enormity of his crime, and the staggering number of years over which it was perpetrated, Josef Fritzl is indeed a cellblock Lucifer. The prisoner who gets to harm him would find himself fêted among the murderers, robbers, thieves and drug dealers resident in St Poelten jail.

In the early days of his imprisonment, Fritzl thrashed between arrogance and denial, guilt and sorrow, before choosing to give an interview to his lawyer, Rudolf Mayer. He hoped his words would somehow mitigate his circumstances, maintaining he acted out of love in imprisoning Elisabeth.

Mayer has himself been on the receiving end of public outrage due to his decision to defend what the public sees as the indefensible. He said: 'I'm getting letters saying

I should be locked up together with Fritzl. But I'm not representing a monster; I'm representing a human being. As I first saw him, the Latin term "paterfamilias" came to mind. It was used to describe the absolute head of the family – caring, but strict. Nowadays people would call that a patriarch.'

It was Mayer who became the conduit for Fritzl to get his version of events to the outside world. He talked about the complicated electronic devices used to seal Elisabeth's concrete prison. He confirmed the lies he told to police and social workers to mask his acts. He spoke of the hundreds of miles he travelled in order to buy groceries, medicines and clothes for his victim and her children, making sure he would not be seen by anyone who knew him.

And he spoke of the insatiable urge to have sex with her that he succumbed to one year after he imprisoned her. It is a confession, mea culpa, justification, apology and undoubted catharsis. What comes across most strongly in his words is the chilling, cold-hearted, calculating side to his nature. It also reveals his mother-fixation, every bit as strong as that which gripped Norman Bates in Hitchcock's *Psycho*.

It needs no further comment; the world has already decided what he is. Austrian justice must decide what will become of him.

The Confession

'It was an obsession.

'I come from a small family and grew up in a tiny flat in Amstetten. My father was somebody who was a waster; he never took responsibility and was just a loser who always cheated on my mother. When I was four she quite rightly threw him out of the house. After that my mother and I had no contact with this man, he didn't interest us; suddenly there was only us two.

'My mother was a strong woman, she taught me discipline and control and the values of hard work. She sent me to a good school so that I could learn a good trade and she worked really hard, and took a very difficult job to keep our heads above water.

'When I say she was hard on me, she was only as hard as was necessary. She was the best woman in the world. I suppose you could describe me as her man, sort of. She was the boss at home and I was the only man in the house.

'It's complete rubbish to say my mother sexually abused me, my mother was respectable, extremely respectable. I loved her across all boundaries. I was totally in awe of her. Completely and totally in awe. That didn't mean there was anything else between us, though; there never was and there never would have been.'

Asked by his lawyer if he had ever fantasized about a relationship with his mother, he pauses in the dialogue and thinks for a long time before answering.

'Yes, probably. But I was a very strong man, probably

as strong as my mother, and as a result I was able to keep my desires under control. I became older and that meant that when I went outside I managed to meet other women. I had affairs with a few girls and then a short while later I met Rosemarie.'

Asked if Rosemarie had anything in common with his mother, he says: 'Absolutely nothing. She had nothing in common with my mother – well, perhaps there were a few similarities if I really think about it. I mean, Rosemarie was also a wonderful woman, is a wonderful woman. She's just a lot shyer and weaker than my mother.

'I chose her because I had a strong desire then to have lots of children. I wanted children who didn't grow up like me as single children; I wanted children who always had someone else at their side to play with and to support.

'The dream of a big family was with me from when I was very, very small. And Rosemarie seemed to be the perfect mother to realize that dream. This is not a good reason to marry, but it is also true to say that I loved her and I still love her.'

Asked how it happened that, in 1967, after having four children with his wife whom he loved, he had then betrayed her by climbing into a flat and raping a young nurse, he says: 'I don't know what drove me to do that . . . It's really true, I don't know why I did it, I always wanted to be a good husband and a good father.' After 18 months in jail he went back to his wife and had three other children with her.

Despite the testimony claims from neighbours that he was a brutal tyrant at home, Fritzl continues: 'I always put a lot of value on good behaviour and respect, I admit that. The reason for this is that I belong to an old school of thinking that just doesn't exist today.

'I grew up in the Nazi times, and that meant there needed to be control and the respect for authority. I suppose I took some of these old values with me into later life, all subconsciously of course. Yet, despite that, I'm not the monster that I'm portrayed as in the media.'

Asked how he would describe someone who kidnapped his own daughter and locked her in the cellar for 24 years, subjecting her to a brutal regime and repeated rape, he says: 'On the face of it, probably as a monster.'

One point on which he disagrees with his daughter is that he had not assaulted her as a child, saying: 'That's not true. I'm not a man who has sex with little children. I only had sex with her later, much later. It was when she was in the cellar by then, when she'd been in the cellar for a long time.'

It's important to remember that Fritzl's confession has a very specific purpose; to make him appear as reasonable as possible. The doctors and police say they have no cause to believe that Elisabeth would need to lie in order to place her father in a bad light.

Asked if much planning had gone into the crime, Fritzl says: 'Two, three years beforehand, that's true. I guess it must have been around 1981 or 1982 when I began to build a room in my cellar as the cell for her. I got a really heavy concrete and steel door that worked with an electric motor and a remote control, which I used to get into the cellar.

'It needed a number code to open and close. I then plastered the walls, added something to wash in and a small toilet, a bed and a cooking ring, as well as the fridge, electricity and lights.

'Perhaps some people did notice what I was doing, but they really didn't care; why should they? The cellar of my house at the end of the day is my house, it belongs to me, it is my kingdom that only I can enter. That's what everyone knew who lived in the area. That includes my wife, my children, and my tenants, and none of them ever managed to force their way into my kingdom or asked me what I did there. I made it clear that this was my office, with various files and folders stored that only had anything to do with me, and that was enough – everybody obeyed my rules.

'Ever since she entered puberty Elisabeth stopped doing what she was told; she just didn't follow any of my rules any more. She would go out all night in local bars, and come back stinking of alcohol and smoke. I tried to rescue her from the swamp and I organized a trainee job for her as a waitress, but sometimes there were days when she wouldn't go to work. She even ran away twice and hung around with persons of questionable moral standards, who were certainly not a good influence on her. I always had to bring her home, but she always ran away again. That's why I had to arrange a place where I gave her the chance – by force – to keep away from the bad influences of the outside world.'

Fritzl denies handcuffing his daughter and keeping her on a lead in the early days of her incarceration. 'That wasn't necessary; my daughter had no chance to get away anyway.'

On that much, at least, they agree: Elisabeth has said

she screamed and banged on the walls but nobody came. Gradually she had to accept that nobody other than her father could help and she should do as he said or she would never again see the light of day. She wrote letters to her family, at her father's command, telling them of a new life and that she had no desire to return; she asked them not to look for her. Her mother, her brothers and sisters and the officials believed the fiction, and the search was wound down.

The master of the cellar knew he was safe: 'I guess after the kidnap I got myself in a vicious circle, a vicious circle not just for Elisabeth but also for me from which there was no way out. With every week that I kept my daughter prisoner my situation just got more crazy – and really, it's true, I often wondered if I should set her free or not. But I just wasn't capable of making a decision, even though, and probably because, I knew that every day made my crime that much worse.

'I was scared of being arrested, and that my family and everybody who knew me would know my crime. That was why I kept putting off the day I should make a decision, putting it off again and again. Eventually, after a time, it was just too late to bring Elisabeth back into the world.

'My desire to have sex with Elisabeth also got much stronger as time went by. We first had sex in spring 1985. I couldn't control myself any more. At some stage somewhere in the night I went into the cellar and lay her down on the bed and had sex with her.'

Every two or three days he went into the cellar, to bring her foodstuffs and clothes and blankets, and told her of his life outside, his work with property, and of her mother who was so sad about the daughter who had run away. He told her how the garden was growing, and about films on the television and trips he had made, and how well her brothers and sisters were doing in school. He admits that he took advantage of his helpless daughter and repeatedly had sex. 'It was an obsession with me,' he says.

She became pregnant the first time in 1988: 'Elisabeth was of course very worried about the future, but I brought her medical books in the cellar, so that she'd know when the day came what she had to do, and I arranged towels and disinfectants and nappies.'

In 1989 Elisabeth gave birth to Kerstin, alone in the cellar. Likewise, Stefan was also born, alone and unaided, in 1990.

'I was delighted about the children. It was great for me to have a second proper family in the cellar, with a wife, and a few children.'

Asked what would have happened if he'd been killed in a car accident, he says: 'I prepared well for this eventuality. Every time I left the bunker I switched on a timer that would definitely have opened the door to the cellar after a set time. If I had died, Elisabeth and the children would have been free.' This was a lie: police discovered that no such timing device existed.

In 1992 Lisa was born, and screamed so much and was frequently so ill that Fritzl decided he needed to take charge of the situation with the cellar family; he arranged for her to be released into the outside world. On 18 May, 1993, Elisabeth wrote the letter that would introduce her daughter to her family.

'Elisabeth and I planned everything together, because we both knew that Lisa, because of her poor health condition and the circumstances in the cellar, had no chance to live had she remained there.'

The same situation applies to Monika, born in 1994, and Alexander, born in 1996. Both were from the beginning of their lives 'weak, difficult, and often ill'. Fritzl says there were 'complications' caused by their arrival that he did not want to deal with – and upstairs, in any case, they would be safe with Rosemarie, who was 'the best mother in the world'.

Both knew she would care for the children. The bizarre double life continued over the years with Rosemarie upstairs, caring for the official family; she did not complain about his sex holidays in Thailand, but cooked, washed and remained faithful to him. Meanwhile, in the cellar downstairs, his second 'wife', as he describes Elisabeth, was kept eternally secret. He says she 'was just as good a housewife and mother'.

Fritzl confirms that an unexpected side effect of the children was that, with every new baby, he gained more control over his daughter. Her own life had no longer become important to her, but she had every reason to do everything he wanted, for the sake of her children. In return he would bring her photographs and stories of the life of the children upstairs, playing games, birthday parties and later on school trips.

In 1993 he expanded the underground bunker into another two rooms. He says he wanted to extend his 'kingdom'. He brought a television and radio into the cellar, as well as a video recorder, table, chairs, carpets, cupboards, plates, tables and pots. He also brought more kitchen utensils and coloured pictures to put on the walls.

'After the birth of Felix, at the end of 2002, I even gave Elisabeth a washing machine as a present so that she didn't have to wash her own clothes and those of the children by hand.

'I always knew over 24 years that what I did wasn't correct, and that I must be mad, to do something like this. Yet despite that, at the same time, it just became a matter of course that I lived my second life in the cellar.'

Upstairs, the three children he had with Elisabeth called him 'Daddy' even though they knew he was their grandfather, whereas downstairs his three children used to call him grandfather.

The pictures on the television were from another planet. And Elisabeth never ever spoke of how much she was suffering to her children. She never screamed or fought when he assaulted her, and taught her children always to 'be nice' to grandfather. They survived in the stinking mould-infested cellar as she fought to keep a perfect house, with clean rooms. She made sure her children were washed every day and ate as well as they could in the circumstances. In the interests of the children she played games.

'I tried really hard, as much as possible, to look after my family in the cellar. When I went there I brought my daughter flowers and the children books and cuddly toys. I used to watch videos and adventure stories with them, while Elisabeth used to cook for me and the children; we used to sit at the table then with each other. We celebrated birthdays and Christmas in the cellar – I even brought a Christmas tree secretly into the cellar, and cakes and presents.'

Despite his surface affections, Fritzl admits that the cellar environment badly affected the health of his daughter and incest brood.

'Yeah, sure, Elisabeth stayed strong, she caused me almost no problems, she never ever complained, even when her teeth slowly went rotten and fell out of her mouth one after the other, and she suffered day and night with unbearable pain and couldn't sleep. She stayed strong for the children, but the children – I saw they were constantly getting weaker.'

The emotional stress of being locked up – and the inability to get out and move in freedom, together with the bad air from the poorly ventilated cellar and the mould on the walls – affected all three children. More and more often, admits Fritzl, they suffered from infections including flu, strong coughing attacks and heart and circulation problems. There were also epileptic fits.

He brought medicine, but none of it was prescription medicine – it was all potions and lotions that he could get over the counter of an ordinary chemist without any questions asked. The most common was aspirin – a drug which, ironically, can be fatal under certain circumstances to children. Fritzl used it as a cure-all for every problem in the dungeon. The aspirin did not help – the children had inherited, from their grandmother, an allergy to it. Felix and Kerstin seem to have suffered the most.

Asked if he wanted to finally release them, he says: 'I wanted to free Elisabeth, Kerstin, Stefan and Felix and to bring them back home; that was my next step. The reason is that I was getting older, I was finding it harder to move and I knew that in the future I would no longer be able to care for my second family in the cellar. The plan was that Elisabeth and the children would explain that they were kept by a sect in a secret place.'

Asked if he thought this was realistic, and that they would not betray him, he says: 'Sure, that was my hope, however unbelievable at that time. Despite that, there was always the risk that Elisabeth and the children would betray me. That did happen rather sooner than I expected as the problem with Kerstin escalated.'

Elisabeth told the police her father had many danger-ous ways of keeping them under control but, when asked how he would stop them escaping, he says: 'It wasn't difficult. I certainly didn't need any physical violence. Elisabeth, Kerstin, Stefan and Felix accepted me as the head of the family completely, and they never trusted themselves to have the strength to attack me. And, in any case, only I knew the number code of the remote control that would open the door to the cellar and close it.'

He denies saying that they would be gassed if they tried to break out, but admits: 'I'm sorry to say that I did tell them that they'd never get past the door because they'd be electrocuted and they'd die.'

Asked if he wants to die, he says: 'No, I only want one thing now: to pay for what I did.'

Lesley Perman-Kerr, a prominent British consultant psy-chologist based in St Albans, believes that Fritzl's later controlling behaviour may have its roots in the strict discipline instilled by his mother Maria. Dr Perman-Kerr, who has worked with kidnap and abuse victims, says: 'All human beings have a dark side and are capable of doing monstrous things. Usually we manage to suppress our darker side through our social and cultural boundaries.

'But power corrupts, and Josef had too much power in his family and no one to challenge him. Also, he had the strict and cruel "moral" code from his mother, which gave him the "permission" to act in particular ways and "discipline" his daughter.

'There seems also to be a very strong sexual motive running through the relationship with his mother. I'm sure he is telling the truth when he says he started something that got bigger and more out of control than expected . . . It's difficult to describe him as mad. His mind appears to be structured and he appears organized in his thinking, albeit deluded.

'It's as if he walked through a door, psychologically speaking, to the dark side – rather like the cellar in which he kept daughter Elisabeth and her children. This was a world in which the bizarre and the cruel became the norm. He also admits to knowing what he did was wrong. Madness doesn't have that kind of insight. He may believe he loves his family in that twisted world of his.'

Ultimately, it will not be her analysis of Fritzl that will determine the path of justice he will follow – leading either to maximum security jail or secure psychiatric institution – but a woman called Adelheid Kastner, a forensic psychologist who has been assigned to test his mental credentials. She is reluctant to let much out about him, but does admit: 'My first impression was of course that this case is absolutely unique. Absolutely. And since then, despite intensive searches, I have not found anything comparable. Of course you can mention names like Natascha Kampusch or Marc Dutroux, the man who kept girls in his cellar and raped them. But what makes this case completely unique is the unbelievably long amount of time that was involved.

'Obviously I can't talk about details of my conversations with Josef Fritzl, but I always start any professional examination from a neutral standpoint, and of course a professional one. It's not up to me to make a judgement. I start every fresh interview with the same polite introductions and values, and I expect the same from my interview partner, whoever it is.

'The amazing thing about this case is also the enormous media interest – partly of course because it is without comparison. If the recommendation that I make is not what society expects – for example, over whether he is responsible for his actions because of his mental state – it's not something that bothers me. It's not my job to worry about it.'

Dr Kastner says she has to win the trust of Josef Fritzl in order to be able to make a complete and accurate assessment of his mental state: 'He will not readily reveal his innermost thoughts and feelings, unless I approach him with a very carefully prepared strategy. It's really important to me that I speak to the criminal completely alone. Apart from me and the interviewee no one else will be in the room. Neither am I superficial or unapproachable. Generally of course, I do not give out any private details about my life, but I do make observations

– such as the fact that the traffic was heavy today, or what the weather is like. I separate my private life and my job. That is obvious.

'A criminal offence is usually just a culmination in the development of a person. Many criminals have got very sad histories. That doesn't of course mean that they're not to be punished for their crimes. There are very few cases where people who do something wrong really see themselves as bad.

'There is one that stays in my mind; it was a man from Graz who had an incestuous relationship with his sister and they had several children together. In between, the sister had another relationship which produced a child, and then the incestuous relationship continued again. In the meantime, the brother develops a real hatred of the genetically different child which he abuses to a massive degree, beating him repeatedly around the head and banging him against the wall. The child was beaten almost to death and survived for three days, whimpering with a fractured skull, lying in bed. Eventually the man got fed up with the crying and tied the child to the luggage rack on his cycle together with some stones and threw him in a river. That was the most awful thing I have had to investigate.

'Abuse by parents of their own children is not uncommon because they are victims easily to hand. It's also easy to hide such abuse within the family structure. That is slowly changing in society, because more and more victims are going to the police. Yet, in spite of that, very often victims have a very ambivalent relationship to the abuser. A father who abuses a child nevertheless is a very important person in that child's life, and from a very early time. There is no black and white. Of course such a person causes severe damage to a child, but out of that can come some positive points that make it very difficult to act against the abuser. During the night a father might be abusive, and during the day the perfect role-model father.'

Asked if she agrees with the defence lawyer's claim that he wanted to get to know the real Josef Fritzl, and not the monster portrayed in the press, she says: 'I have never been asked to examine a monster.'

10. Aftermath

The past is a foreign country: they do things differently there.

L. P. Hartley, *The Go-Between*

Austria needs to recover. It needs to recover from, and deal with, the aftermath of the Fritzl case. While it is assumed that he will never live to renovate another cellar in this world – he will spend what time is left to him either in a prison or in a secure psychiatric institution – Austria must have a painful reckoning with its role as arch-enabler in his crimes.

The Amstetten case, coming on top of the Kampusch saga, has given the impression of the Alpine state being less a nation of beauty and culture and more a land peopled by citizens who imprison girls in cellars. They abuse them while their neighbours avoid the warning signs and ugly truths, because they do not want to get involved. Smug officialdom fails – the result of an unhealthy obsession with appearance over reality – and bourgeois good behaviour masks terrible truths.

There have been critics, such as Thomas Glavinic, a noted Austrian author, who has roundly condemned his countrymen: 'The countryside hates everything that is at a distance: the government, the EU, the Americans, the Jews. There are old-boy networks and there is peer pressure. Those who don't work for their local volunteer fire brigade, or at least donate money to their village fête, are branded oddballs or outsiders. The rest, on the other hand, could beat up their wives and kids in their spare time. We wouldn't care. It's just none of our business.'

Josef Haslinger, a philosopher and writer, has said: 'There is this pretty, shiny surface that Austrians like to show, but it hides a monstrosity. On the surface we have moral standards and enlightened policies, but in the background we have this perverse world that nobody wants to talk about. We are still not able to accept our mistakes. So forgetting has become part of the mentality. If you look too closely, you might have to act. So nobody looks.

'My country has the fatal tradition of sweeping things under the carpet. In Austria, private shortcomings and public morality have no connection with each other. The de-Nazification process actually never succeeded. Until decades after the Second World War, we didn't deal with the moral failings of private individuals. There is a dual character. The cheerful face and behind the façade the unspeakable and horrific. That has a real tradition in Austrian art and literature. That is no coincidence. We have a culture of looking away.'

'Elisabeth ran away from that house as a girl, police searched for her, brought her back and delivered her into the violent embrace of her father,' says Hedwig Woelfl, the director of a child protection centre in Austria. 'Running away from home was a clear sign of unhappiness, but nobody apparently showed any interest in the fate of this girl.'

Of course it is true that Austria has no monopoly on horrific crimes. Marc Dutroux in Belgium used a cellar to store his child victims in, as did Fred and Rosemary West in the United Kingdom and mass murderer John Wayne Gacy in America. Yet there is something special about Austria. It is a society wreathed in secrets and denial, especially in modern times. There is a culture of silence, which breeds families locked in their own silences. After the first why-oh-why pieces about Austria appeared in the British press, following the discovery of the cellar, many readers complained, claiming that Fritzl's crime was not the symptom of a sick nation. I would argue otherwise – there is something rotten at the heart of Austria.

At a local level, it was the people of Amstetten who bore the brunt of the media onslaught and the criticism of Austria. It is they who will have to live with the consequences of Austria's societal fault lines for years to come. For, despite the journalistic hyperbole, these fault lines do exist – and they are dangerous. But the citizens of Amstetten, like everyone else, want to forget and not to reflect too much on why Fritzl was allowed to remain in their midst – unlike his victims – unmolested.

On May 7 this year 500 people turned up at the town's main square with twin messages – those of support for Elisabeth and her children, and those urging the world's media to disappear. A banner made by the town's school-children carried messages like: 'Wishing you strength on your path through life'; 'We're with you' and 'It was hell for you, now we wish you lots of sunlight'. But there were other messages, critical of the media and of Austrian society. 'Our society is built on arrogance, ignorance and selfishness,' read one. 'The media is reporting even though it has nothing more to report,' said another.

The rally was organized to show that the town wants to move on. Margarete Reisinger said: 'I'm here because this was one man and it now reflects on all of us. I'm proud to be from Amstetten. The name is mentioned all the time and is now being discredited. We must remember he was not a normal man.'

Robert Schiller, another citizen at the rally, said: 'We in Amstetten can't help that we had such a person among us, but the whole world is watching us.'

The case has been particularly hard to take for Amstetten's schoolchildren, many of whom knew the Fritzls' 'upstairs children'. Margit Schagerl, a teacher at the local school, confirmed: 'It's a huge topic at the moment among the kids. They're all deeply affected.'

City spokesman Hermann Gruber addressed the rally and told the crowd: 'This Amstetten we see today, that's the real Amstetten.'

Unfortunately, Amstetten seems to suffer the same myopia as the rest of the country. Its citizens, undoubtedly ashamed by what occurred, seem intent on shooting the messenger instead of heeding the message: 'How and why?'

Why was Fritzl's rape conviction not taken into account when he was fostering and adopting children? Why did social welfare teams, people whose task it is to act as busybodies, visit the home of a convicted felon 21 times and never take a look around? How could it be that his fantastical story of his daughter joining a cult is given credibility – and then babies start arriving with the regularity of the post on his doorstep and no alarm bells sound anywhere?

Bureaucrats of all stripes were in and out of that house, including building inspectors and fire safety officials. Did none of them have the faintest suspicion of what lay beyond the front door, or in the dark at the foot of the cellar stairs?

Heinz Lenze, the Mayor of Amstetten, said that in 1994, when the first child, Lisa, was adopted, neither Fritzl nor his wife apparently had any criminal convictions. Under Austrian law, Fritzl, the knife-wielding rapist, had done his time and the crime was effectively erased. 'In such cases, giving the child to members of the family is always preferred to committing it to a foster home,' Mr Lenze explains, claiming that social services did not disobey the standard procedures. Asked how it was possible that records of such serious offences as sexual assault and suspected arson had not been kept, he replies: 'I'm only a civil servant and not a lawmaker.'

So is anybody to blame, then? And if so, who? Who will take responsibility?

The Austrian Chancellor, keen to get the mountains, the Sachertorte and the *Sound of Music* meadows back into the minds of potential tourists everywhere, has argued that Fritzl's crime was not uniquely Austrian; that any society anywhere could have thrown up a ghost in the machine, such as happened in Amstetten.

But not even the Austrian media, a tame beast

compared to the press in Britain and the US, buys into that one. 'What society would accept the probability of three children being left on the doorstep of Josef Fritzl over a decade, and grant him adoption rights without enquiring after the location of the mother?' asked one newspaper.

'How is it possible that nobody heard or saw anything, that nobody asked questions?' enquired Petra Stuiber, columnist of *Der Standard* in Vienna. 'What does this say about neighbours and the extended family, acquaintances and, above all, civil servants dealing with the family? A whole country has to ask itself what is going fundamentally wrong.'

Austrians pride themselves on what they call their 'social partnership' form of society, but while it may have served them well economically, it has created the vacuum in which Fritzl and Priklopil were able to operate. This role model of living was founded after the devastation of the Second World War, when the government, as well as industry and the trade unions, collectively decided the country could not afford to repeat the destructive social, political and economic conflict that marked the 1920s and 1930s, when the country lurched from one crisis to another culminating in the Anschluss of 1938. They wanted to avoid ruinous social and industrial conflict, strikes, lock-outs, and the kind of persistent social battles that had contributed to the paralysis of the Austrian economy and its governments during the interwar years. It means a virtually strike-free society, one where deals are hammered out behind closed doors, one where people don't rock the boat, where union bosses do deal with industrialists, politicians with politicians, financiers with financiers. Often in secret.

Austrians don't like harking back to the Nazis – for them it is long ago and far away. Historically, it is yesterday, and it is as near as the neighbours were to Josef Fritzl's front door. His story starts and ends with the Nazis whose philosophy was so deeply attractive to the boy Josef as he grew up. It ends with them because Austria truly has never had a reckoning with them, and with its relationship to them. To comprehend why the Nazis still cast their shadow across the country it is only necessary to read up on one Dr Heinrich Gross. He was another man who was fond of his cellar, where he kept his own particular secrets. And the Austrian state, particularly its movers and shakers, were happy to keep them too.

Heinrich Gross was 90 when he died, having skilfully avoided justice for nearly 60 years at the same time as society heaped awards upon him. He was rarely out of the spotlight. The good doctor became the leading forensic authority in criminal trials. As such, he was often on television and seated at the tables of the rich, the famous and the influential in Viennese society. Witty, meticulously spoken, a man who held his drink well, Dr Gross was considered entertaining, charming, amusing. His hosts, and his patrons in government, chose to ignore his wicked past where he earned the nickname 'The Scythe'. His particular crop: defenceless children. Murdered in their scores for the advancement of the Aryan master race. Gross worked at the Am Spiegelgrund children's hospital in Vienna in 1944, where he was complicit in the murders of hundreds of children deemed to be 'unworthy of life'. Long after the guns fell silent, it was found he had kept the brains of his child victims in a private collection in his cellar, using them for experiments as recently as the 1970s. Lined up in formaldehyde preserving fluid, like dolls in aspic, the children's remains were finally laid to rest in 2002.

Dr Gross managed to escape prosecution until 1950, when he was sentenced to two years in prison for being an accessory to a single case of manslaughter. But the verdict was later overturned by the high court. He joined the Social Democratic Party and went on to become one of the country's leading neurologists and its second highest-earning doctor. The case against Gross was reopened after new evidence came to light in the mid 1990s, including declassified papers from the East German secret police archives. In February 1998 prosecutors removed 400 brains from Dr Gross's private collection. Experiments carried out by doctors in Innsbruck found that nine of the brains of children aged between 10 days and 14 years old showed traces of poison – the remnants of sleeping tablets administered by Dr Gross. In most cases pneumonia was stated as the cause of death.

In 2000, former child victims who survived Spiegelgrund, along with relatives of the dead, packed room 203 of Vienna's criminal court to watch as Dr Gross, dressed in a cloth cap and grey suit, shuffled slowly to the witness stand, accompanied by his doctor, where he played the 'Pinochet Card' – unfit to stand trial.

His head was bowed as Judge Karlheinz Seewald asked him: 'Can you understand me?'

Dr Gross answered: 'Not very well.'

Reinhard Haller, a doctor who examined Dr Gross twice, told the court that his patient was suffering from dementia and that his mental and physical health was deteriorating fast. He said Dr Gross had slight brain damage and showed signs of the initial stages of Parkinson's disease. 'He's not confused; he knows where he is and he knows why he's here.' But because of a reduced attention span and memory lapses, he would have great trouble following the trial for periods of longer than 5 to 10 minutes.

After a short intermission, the judge declared Dr Gross unfit to stand trial, saying: 'Dr Gross's mental and physical health has considerably worsened since the last examination. If he is not able to follow the case, it must be adjourned.'

He got away with murder until the day he died, peacefully, in his bed in December 2005. And what was the Austrian state's highest censure? It took away the medal it gave him.

Germany, post-1945, under the orders of the allied powers that divided and ruled it, ordered citizens and institutions to undergo de-Nazification procedures intended to expunge them of National Socialist thinking and traits. Austria's attempts at purging the 'brown stain' were far more erratic and haphazard. Consequently, the grandfather in post-war Germany became, in the 1960s, a reviled figure. The young wanted to know what the sins of the elders were – as the economic miracle put VWs on the drive and paid for foreign holidays abroad, they wanted to know what Papa and Grandpapa had done on the killing fields of Russia, in Lithuania, in Poland, Greece, Yugoslavia, France, Latvia, Estonia and Holland. In Germany the family secrets spilled out and all men of a certain age were regarded with suspicion. This desire for a truthful confrontation with the past spawned the Baader-Meinhof gang, which sought to destroy a state it said had been built on lies and shame.

In Austria, the grandfathers were, and remain, a revered caste, and the questions that needed to be addressed were not asked. Austria unilaterally branded itself Nazism's first victim, and that was that. It was no accident that one of the first groups the far right politician Joerg Haider spoke to, as he broadened his limited appeal in Carinthia outwards to encompass the whole nation, was a group of Waffen SS veterans. He was giving them the respect he thought they deserved, and he called them honourable men. Austrians never questioned him, but supported him in the face of world revulsion. The country collectively looked away, never asking the most basic questions. Such as how he came to live in a multi-million-pound mansion with saw mills, streams and acres of land.

The answer lies in the Nazi past: it was dispossessed from a Jewish family and sold at a knock-down price so the family could escape. Haider feels no shame in living in such a house, where the moral mortgage will forever outweigh any fiscal debt that may be owed. Yet the electorate preferred to look the other way, electing his party to power despite the scorn of the world.

Nor do they sit easy with the Simon Wiesenthal Centre in Israel's assertion that their land is a 'haven' for Nazi war criminals. Dr Efraim Zuroff, director of the centre

devoted to bringing to justice the remaining living criminals of the Nazi regime, has denounced Austria as guilty
of 'consistent failures' in bringing Nazis in its midst to
justice. He is particularly incensed over Vienna's refusal
to extradite Milivoj Asner back to Croatia. Asner, who
currently resides in Klagenfurt, in Austria, served as police
chief of Pozega, Croatia, during the Second World War
and played an important role in the persecution and
murder of hundreds of Jews, Serbs and gypsies. He was
exposed by the Wiesenthal Centre's 'Operation: Last
Chance' project, a bid to round up the remaining killers.

'It's very simple,' says Zuroff. 'We're determined to
bring these bastards to trial. These people don't deserve
any sympathy – they killed Jews, gypsies, gays, Jehovah's
Witnesses and many other people just for being who they
were. But we're up against some serious obstacles in
countries like Austria where there is a complete lack of
political will to prosecute Nazi war criminals. Vienna
hasn't sentenced anyone for Holocaust war crimes in
three decades. Do you think it's because there are no war
criminals there? Hardly. There are many there. But Austria
has shown no interest or serious activity to bring them
to justice. There is a system here that makes Austria a
paradise for Nazi war criminals, plain and simple.'

In 1985 I journeyed to Vienna to meet Wiesenthal
himself, the living legend, the scourge of old Nazis everywhere. The man who lost 89 members of his family in
the Holocaust could have based his agency tracking down
the guilty anywhere. He could have gone to Bonn and
been near the prosecutors assigned to finding them, or
to New York where Jewish money would have been more

easily accessible to fund his efforts. He chose to stay in Vienna for this reason: 'I stayed here because I was a thorn in their sides and their conscience . . . these good, bourgeois Austrians who bleated that they were the victims of Nazism. They embraced it with a vengeance. I prick their consciences daily – that is why I stayed.' He played a prominent role in exposing the late Austrian president Kurt Waldheim's less than honourable wartime role as a German army officer on duty in the Balkans, where massacres of partisans and unarmed civilians were the order of the day.

Waldheim, who also served ten years as Secretary-General of the United Nations, did his best to keep the details of these times secret too. This is the seamless link between individuals like Fritzl and the Austrian mentality.

Every family has secrets; they do not need to be on the catastrophic level of a Josef Fritzl, but they exist. Ally such secrets to a state that also keeps them, and it becomes easier to see why Austria does have a problem. It is with the Nazis as backdrop that Fritzl felt able to carry out his plan to incarcerate his daughter in the first place; in staying out late and drinking and smoking, she not only rebelled against his personal code, but against the whole of his life and the society in which he believed and which shaped him. She wouldn't obey – off into the secret cellar with her. He knew his secret would be safe; after all, he called it his 'kingdom'. He knew because he knew his fellow Austrians, and his judgement was proved correct.

Fritzl and his wife, a devout Catholic – which makes one wonder what she said in confession – grew up in a different era, with clear separation of roles. Feminists may dismiss the social attitudes of the 1940s and 50s as Stone Age sexism: man as the hunter-gatherer; woman as the dutiful spouse who doesn't ask questions and stays in the kitchen. But such attitudes are part of the texture of Austrian society. Men were not only allowed to have parallel lives, they were expected to: Austrian men of a certain age classically had a girlfriend in another village. Fritzl almost certainly did too – not to mention his secret family downstairs. If his wife didn't think to question him about his movements, why should his neighbours ask questions? After all, a man has a right to a secret or two.

Rosemarie was respected in the community. Why? Because she brought up her daughter's children as if they were her own. She never complained in public about Josef. The kids were always taken punctually to music classes, football and other activities, were always smartly turned out.

But it was all surface stuff. No one thought – or dared – to poke beneath the surface because that is not the Austrian way.

Austrian politicians have promised a review of all the facts in the Fritzl case. But there exists a blueprint for official lethargy, for lessons not learned or mistakes not heeded, as witnessed in the Kampusch case. Two years on from her re-entry into the world of light, officialdom has done little to address the grave mishaps in her case.

The police failings in the hunt for her when she disappeared as a 10-year-old schoolgirl are legendary, such as the failure to search the home of suspect – and perpetrator – Wolfgang Priklopil with dogs that would have immediately picked up Natascha's scent. Then there was the failure to take his photograph to show to witnesses who saw the little girl getting into a white van of the sort he owned, added to the fact that no psychological profile of the potential kidnapper was ever commissioned. The case officers worked for the first nine months without an effective computer system linked to Interpol, or even to other Austrian forces. In the end, they resorted to hiring pendulum twiddlers and ouija board shufflers in a bid to find her. Max Edelbacher was head of the taskforce charged with finding her at the time, and only went into retirement the month before Natascha escaped. He says: 'Nobody, not me nor any other policeman, believed she could still be alive. However, it's horrible that a girl could be held in our area for eight years while being unsuccessfully searched for by thousands of policemen. Questions, rightly, must be asked about where we went wrong.'

In February, 2008, Herwig Haidinger, former head of the Federal Criminal Police Office, revealed that Priklopil had indeed been exposed as a key suspect in the Kampusch enquiry within weeks of the girl's vanishing. But he was dealt with in a four-minute doorstep interview and was then free to groom, molest, corrupt and defile his victim over the next eight and a half years. At the time of writing, a parliamentary commission called to investigate the failings of the police – fuelled in part by a detective breaking ranks to claim that the original probe was botched from the start and the failings covered up to prevent a scandal – has reported that grave mistakes were indeed made. Given the cosy, intertwining interests of the judiciary and the political scene in Austria, those hoping for breathtaking changes may be in for a long wait. It is not known if the commission will address the revelations of a newspaper investigation, published in Vienna earlier in 2008, which indicates that police held back evidence of Kampusch's diary, notes from Priklopil, and photos and videos which suggest Priklopil may have had accomplices. The leads were not pursued by police and were sealed by prosecutors in 2006. It is as if they had been covered in lead and concrete and sunk with the waste from Chernobyl into some bottomless pit, never to be disturbed.

Furthermore, peculiar privacy laws in Austria dictate that newspapers and magazines in Kampusch's homeland are intimidated by her lawyers into suppressing any speculation about what took place during her captivity. People in her homeland are forbidden from questioning the precise nature of her victimhood.

There is yet another case of wicked child abuse that was allowed to continue for many years, undoubtedly due to the inbuilt cap-doffing nature that Austrians have towards authority. It too involved a cellar, darkness, seclusion and an outside world turning away. And, as in the cases of Natascha Kampusch, and Elisabeth Fritzl and her children, the victims will bear the scars for ever and will never know complete normality again in their lives. Three girls were imprisoned in a house of 'indescribable filth' for seven years by their demented mother who became unhinged. The girls were shut away from the outside world, existing in almost complete darkness, playing only with mice in the cellar and communicating in their own made-up language. When they were discovered, their home in a smart, upper-middle-class suburb had no running water and was filled with waste and excrement a metre high. The floor was corroded by mice urine. The case stunned Austria when it broke just months after Natascha's escape. The authorities in Linz, a town where Josef Fritzl enjoyed himself in bordellos and bars, struggled to explain how such a horror story could have gone unnoticed. They are still struggling.

The girls' ordeal was apparently sparked by their parents' divorce in 1998 after which their mother, a 53-year-old lawyer, suffered a breakdown. But she won custody of the girls – then aged 7, 11 and 13 – and withdrew them from school, claiming that she would give them private tuition at home. Her husband, a local judge in Linz, Upper Austria, named only as Andreas M, was not allowed to see them once, despite his claims for access reaching court nine times. The girls were rescued only when police broke into the house after a neighbour, who had reported his suspicions several times, threatened a local council official with a lawsuit. And this over the antics of the family Labrador, not out of concern for the children. The poor beast, driven mad in a house of filth, darkness and dysfunction, distressed the neighbour sufficiently to pick up the telephone when the dog broke through the heavy blackout curtains to throw himself wildly against the glass in a fruitless bid for 'walkies' in an outside world.

Although that was in October 2005, and the three have been in a special therapy centre since, the scandal was

only revealed at the start of 2007. The mother ensured
that the blinds were constantly shut, and that all but one
light bulb had been removed in the house. When they
were released, the three victims had white skin and could
not endure exposure to natural light. The authorities are
now under fire for failing to have intervened sooner,
despite repeated complaints by neighbours in the well-
to-do Poestlingberg area.

The mother was said to have been summoned to court
nine times during the seven years after complaints by the
father and neighbours, but officials never found a reason
to investigate the case more closely. Waltraud Kubelka, a
therapist treating the three girls, said that their psycho-
social and physical development was 'catastrophic'. 'The
oldest one is doing very badly and has no prospects of
recovery. She was severely undernourished and practically
anorexic after her release. The two younger ones will need
years to come to terms with their horrific childhood. In
the first weeks after their release they were hiding under
a bench in the kitchen in the therapy centre because that
was the darkest spot. They could not endure light . . .
they had not felt sunlight or fresh air for years.'

The children had contact only with their mother during
the seven years of captivity and, as a consequence, developed an almost unintelligible language of their own,
described as a 'singing-like' form of German. Even after
a year of therapy the oldest daughter, now 21, is said to
be so disturbed that she stands flamingo-like on one foot
for long periods, staring at the floor. She often bursts
into tears. She and her two sisters also reportedly finish
all sentences with the word 'but'. A council official said

that authorities had had no knowledge of the 'truly cata-strophic' conditions. The mother's legal training and knowledge of the law has reportedly enabled her to post-pone the trial.

Here was the dark side of Austria portrayed once more at its worst. The woman was a judge, therefore a woman of standing. Even when she was seen by some neighbours taking meals in her car parked outside the house, and the police were informed of her strange ways, no action was taken. It is almost as if Austrians are born with a gene that does not permit them to question those who are perceived to be upright citizens. At the time of writing, no police officer or social worker has been called to account. The Linz children seem to be just three more victims of a society that doesn't want to get involved.

It is not just outsiders playing bar-room philosophers with the perceived deficiencies of the Austrian character and state. Austrians themselves are all too aware of their country's role in 20th-century history, how they under-wrote two German-led world wars, lost an empire and fell, happily, into bed with the most wicked regime on the planet. They are just as shocked and disgusted as anyone abroad as to how these recent cases of abuse could have happened, and they concede that certain 'psycho-cultural' elements of their society may have played a role.

Austrian novelist Elfriede Jelinek, winner of the 2004 Nobel Prize for Literature, is a Marxist feminist whose novels have often dealt with the fabric of societies as ruled by the masculine male, depicted as a beast in his private life but outwardly respectable, upstanding, correct (step forward Josef Fritzl), the propagator of society's values. In one book she describes a married couple whose tranquil outer appearance conceals the daily acts of rape and violence the husband perpetrates against his spouse. Jelinek has suggested that it is a combination of Austrian society's patriarchal values, which respect the man in control of his woman, combined with the 'looking away' culture and society's need for harmony that make it possible for such a man to enact his fantasies.

The *Standard* newspaper ran an editorial discussing virility and manliness when neighbours of Fritzl described him as 'a man's man' who seemed highly virile and dominant. The argument ran that this type of man is still respected in Austria, a traditionally Catholic and patriarchal society. An editorial in *Die Presse* pointed to the country's attitude towards parenting and children, which places the ultimate authority on the man as head of the family. Perhaps this explains how Fritzl was able to officially 'adopt' the children he fathered with his daughter.

The finger-pointing and dissection of the Austrian character and its Nazi shadow will go on long after Josef Fritzl is safely locked away, or dead. At the time of writing prosecutors are still arguing over just what to charge him with. They are trying to nail down every single legal loophole that he may try to make use of in order to escape his long-awaited day in court.

What concerns the world is how Austria will deal with what Fritzl did – and society enabled. The first signs are that the old habits are dying hard. Within days of the case making global headlines, Austrian police were accused of trying to stop criticism of their investigation by threatening to sue anyone who spoke to the media about the case. Prosecutors said they planned to take legal action against people who revealed 'intimate details' of the case from their own experiences. They warned that people who 'gave out' information about the Fritzl clan could be violating the family's privacy rights and that giving interviews could lead to prosecutions. Again, it's a case of 'shoot the messenger'.

Former Fritzl tenant Josef Leitner, quoted earlier, states: 'It's nothing but an attempt to cover up facts that might expose failings in their work. I and my family have been intimidated by police after I spoke out that all was not well in that house. I decided to speak after I saw the way they'd already made up their minds about things. It wasn't an easy decision because I know I wasn't in the right in my silence before. Yet rather than looking into what I've said, they just want to shut me up.

'She ran away on more than one occasion. I'm surprised the authorities didn't investigate more intensively. Why didn't they try to find out why Elisabeth wanted to run away again and again? If they'd asked her friends, I'm sure they would have told them.' Leitner says the police have now threatened to report him to the state prosecutor, believing the threat might frighten off other informants. He adds: 'As always, the Austrian authorities are only worried about having a clean record, so they try to pass the blame on to someone else.'

Yet the cosy establishment that strived to accept no blame for Kampusch and for the feral children of Linz may finally be facing an electorate that is no longer as passive as it once was. A huge majority of Austrians believe that the authorities made 'grave mistakes' in the Amstetten case. Claims by the authorities that their work was in order were 'completely inappropriate and implausible' said almost 90 per cent of those interviewed in a survey taken in the weeks following the discovery of the chamber and the secret family within.

Only 10.6 per cent believe the local authorities did everything possible to find Elisabeth, while a total of 93.1 per cent said Amstetten's authorities 'neglected proper checks' when they gave three of Elisabeth's children into Josef Fritzl's care after they were abandoned on his doorstep. Just over 90 per cent agreed that the authorities had put the interests of the potential offender before the victims' rights. Only 5.3 per cent believed that neither police nor neighbours and friends noticed anything strange in Fritzl's behaviour.

Those sentiments have been echoed by Justice Minister Maria Berger, who had said local authorities had been too 'gullible', believing Fritzl's story that his daughter had run away to join an obscure religious sect. Berger says the police were too easily fooled into accepting Fritzl's account that his daughter ran away to join a cult. 'Looking at everything that we know up to now, I can see a certain gullibility – especially when it comes to that tale that she had joined a sect, with which the suspect explained the disappearance of his daughter. I'm certain that such an account would have been more closely examined if presented to the authorities today.'

In one parliamentary debate, the then Interior Minister, Guenther Platter, blasted the crime as the 'most disgusting crime I can remember'. Both he and Berger have vowed to pass stricter legislation against sexual offenders. Maximum sentences will be raised and, in the case of severe sex crimes, deletion of the crime from police registers will be abolished. Ministers have also announced plans to strengthen obligations to report potential abuse cases, to lengthen probation periods, and to introduce a register for sexual offenders plus a ban on them working in certain jobs. People found guilty of prolonged domestic violence and sexual abuse will also face stricter sentences of up to 20 years in prison.

The new legislation is expected to be in force by 2009. Meanwhile, in the aftermath of the shockwaves caused by the Fritzl case, Austrian Chancellor Alfred Gusenbauer has promised new measures that aim to prevent children becoming victims of abuse. 'In the question of violence against children, there can be no compromises,' he says, adding that convicted sex criminals should not be allowed to either adopt children or work with young people. Gusenbauer has also pledged that, in future, criminal records of sex offenders will be held on file for a much longer period, doubling to 30 years, and that serious offences will remain permanently on the books.

All of this comes too late to help Elisabeth and her children but it might, just might, indicate that Austria recognizes that there is a problem – that *Austria* has a problem – and is on the road to doing something about it. Whether that will ever translate into heads rolling and individuals being called to account for their actions – and inactions – remains to be seen.

Epilogue: Travellers in the Land Without Maps

1 June, 2008

Kerstin Fritzl, a woman who had known only four people in the whole of the 19 years she had been alive – her mother, brothers Stefan and Felix, and of course her jailer – woke up to find a fifth person whispering to her.

'Hello,' said the voice.

'Hello,' replied Kerstin.

It was contact in a world she thought she would never see.

After weeks of hovering between life and death in an artificially induced coma – so gravely ill she was even given the last rites by the family priest – the firstborn child of Elisabeth was back.

The greeting came from Dr Albert Reiter, the man who had made everything possible. As she turned her head around, her eyes focused on a person she had only ever seen before in the subterranean setting: her mother.

It would be hard not to imagine the relief Elisabeth must have felt to see her daughter awake and to be able to reassure her they were not going back to the cellar.

And then they both wept.

Kerstin was moved from the Amstetten Hospital to the clinic to rejoin her family as the endgame of their ordeal came into play. In July, 2008, Elisabeth gave a series of interviews via a video link about her ordeal. For four days, seated next to her lawyer, she spoke into a video camera which relayed her testimony to a judge, a prosecutor and her father's lawyer in an adjoining room. She chronicled the abuse she had suffered as a child, the whole terrible saga of the cellar and how it came to end. She also hammered home a point on which she is certain, and which she would like to see used against Fritzl at his trial: namely that he, by his actions and inaction in failing to get medical attention, was responsible for the death in the cellar of her baby boy, Michael. On this she has been most emphatic; she holds him entirely responsible. Her accusations are to be studied by medical and legal experts to see if they can be used to formulate a murder or manslaughter charge against Fritzl.

Fritzl had the right to sit in on the hearing but chose to remain in his cell. For Elisabeth the ordeal will spare her the agony of ever seeing him again; she will not have to be called as a witness at his trial. As prosecutors deliberate on what to charge him with, her words will guarantee that the full horror of what he perpetrated against her over those 8,516 days will never be forgotten.

But Elisabeth may not be the only one with a case to pursue against Fritzl. Police officers are now journeying into the past to discover if, stretching back to the years before he imprisoned and then inflicted such hideous and prolonged abuse on his daughter, Fritzl the convicted rapist might also have been Fritzl the killer.

Anna Neumayer was murdered in August 1966. She was killed with a bolt gun at the age of 17. Her body was discovered in a maize field in Raasdorf in Lower Austria on 25 August, 1966, three days after her disappearance was reported in the town of Pfaffstaett, on her way to the city of Wels in Upper Austria – less than 30 kilometres away from Linz, where Fritzl worked at the time. Police say the perpetrator was about the same age as Fritzl at the time. He was not quizzed about it.

Martina Posch was murdered in November 1986. The 17-year-old girl was found on the shores of the Mondsee lake. She had been strangled then raped. Her body was thrown into the water after it had been hidden for several days. Martina Posch looked surprisingly similar to Elisabeth. The clothes she was wearing at the time of her murder were never found.

Julia Kuehrer went missing on 27 June, 2006, aged 16 at the time. Investigators said the last leads they had on her were in her hometown of Pulkau in Lower Austria but that they had not been able to trace her from there. She remains a missing person.

Gabriele Superkova was murdered in August 2007. She worked as a prostitute at the Austrian/Czech border. Her body was found at the Moldaustausee lake at a time when Fritzl was on vacation in the area.

The police are re-examining these and other crimes – they have even appealed for possible victims of Fritzl to contact them after one woman claimed he had raped her one month before he carried out the rape for which he was convicted and subsequently jailed in 1968. The unnamed 61-year-old woman from Linz said she was attacked in September 1967 by Fritzl, at the age of 20. She was quoted in the local media as saying: 'I was also raped by this man but I was too embarrassed to report it to the police. Please don't give out my name but I'm 100 per cent sure it was Fritzl.'

Court spokesman Gerhard Sedlaczek has appealed for the woman and any other possible victims of the serial sex offender Fritzl to get in touch. He says: 'We do not want to miss anything. We have appealed for anyone who may have information to contact us. It would be far more preferable for these people to do this directly through the police or the courts than through the media.'

Now, as Kerstin recovers and dreams of the Robbie Williams concert she wants to attend – she loved his songs while lying half-comatose on her bed in the cellar – she and her siblings are learning, in small steps, the ways of this exciting, daunting new existence. Kerstin's bond with her mother is extraordinary, as is that of her two brothers. Together they survived in the underworld solely thanks to her strength, her inspiration, her unflinching devotion to them.

Stefan and Kerstin, drawn closer by their ages, spend much time together at the clinic. They make plans, talk about places they would like to visit, where they would like to live. How soon those plans will crystallize is as much a mystery to them as to the psychiatric specialists dealing with them. There is so much to learn, from how to interact with others, to learning trust, to not fearing shut doors, to understanding that not all male authority figures lurk with a TV remote control in their fist ready to confine them again. The task is nothing short of Herculean.

Interestingly, both Stefan and Kerstin refused in July

to join their mother in giving testimony against Fritzl. It is unclear whether this is out of a lingering sense of affection, or the result of fear, hatred or pity. Certainly, the confused feelings they have for him – on the one hand, he was their jailer and the abuser of their mother, on the other hand he was the man who brought them food and ultimately saved Kerstin's life – continue to torment them. Nothing is black and white – not for them, not for the therapists. Everything is shaded grey.

Physically, much has improved. Stefan is no longer stooped; his anaemia and vitamin-D deficiences are all but gone. Kerstin will make a full recovery, although she will rely on a cocktail of drugs to control her fits throughout her life.

Felix the joker, the bundle of energy who delights all, is slowly but surely forgetting the past. Doctors hope that, aged five, the cellar for him can recede into some vague place in his psyche where it can disintegrate into something non-threatening, even benign. His development is retarded, but not to the extent of his elder siblings. He can learn to remember things in his bright new world and he can learn to forget the horrors of the past.

The other children, who were raised upstairs, will have their own resentments to nurture. Fed propaganda for all their lives that their mother was worthless, they had carved out life as it should be: loving grandparents, interested teachers, good friends, prospects. At a stroke their world was wiped out. They became 'incest children' overnight and, overnight, were uprooted like refugees from their warm, safe house to a psychiatric clinic where men in white coats pored over them and a woman who was a stranger tried to play catch-up on the lost years. Separated from their pals and their activities, where they go from here is anyone's guess. While they are getting to know their mother, the impact of the emotional wrench from their old lives has been enormous and tortured. They are no doubt confused about their feelings for all their family figures.

The extent of this emotional upheaval manifested itself in the last week of July. Despite the rosy picture of 'two tribes living as one' painted by Christoph Herbst, Elisabeth is at loggerheads with her mother. The issues are on many levels – her passiveness during Elisabeth's upbringing when the girl was being abused, the fact that she stayed with her husband when he was a convicted rapist, the fact that she did not question more earnestly her daughter's disappearance into a 'sect' – but one simple, human failing on the part of the children has brought the issues with Rosemarie to a head.

The upstairs children could not stop calling Rosemarie mother. Elisabeth would chastise them, then chastise Rosemarie for not correcting them more forcefully. It has led, according to media reports in the country at the time of writing, to an almost complete disintegration of the mother–daughter relationship. This, truly, is why they are all navigating their way through a land without maps. This is Josef Fritzl's ultimate legacy: the shattering of lives and familial love, even though he has been removed from the stage.

After Elisabeth's ordeal, with no skills, and no pro-spects, how can she know if the generosity of a state fall-ing over itself to atone for what happened will extend to enough fiscal help to see her through the rest of her life? She wants to remain anonymous but that may not be an option. As Herr Polzer has remarked, in an interview for this book: 'I can't see any option for her but, eventually, to go to the media and to tell her story. She has no way of making enough money to keep six children. I think she will be forced by circumstance, one day, to tell all.'

Until then, she no doubt continues to count her blessings as she watches each sunset and sunrise. She loves all her children, loves her freedom, but she is also a captive in the hospital and a prisoner of her own fears. Paparazzi lurk outside the gates, eager for the million-dollar picture of the 'cellar mum'. And where would she go? Consumerism holds no pleasures for her, any friends she had have grown up and drifted away, there is no one to drop in on for a cup of tea or a slice of cake.

What she has lost is incalculable; what she may regain for a meaningful life is unknown.

The puzzle of what will happen to the Amstetten victims parallels that of the physical site of their suffering. What becomes of the 'House of Horrors' is unclear. The police have bagged and tagged everything within, probed with sonar for secret rooms which don't exist, satisfied themselves that the underworld was no bigger than it actually appeared. Tourists still draw up to the front, point, sometimes take a picture with a digital camera or a mobile phone, but police permanently stationed to keep the press and the obsessively curious rubberneckers at bay say the lure of the macabre is gradually fading.

There was one visitor in early June who was allowed

in, allowed to walk down to see the secret world of Josef Fritzl in all its unique, stultifying madness. She spent 40 minutes down there, gathering up the possessions of the cave children which police had left in their place: the ragged teddy belonging to Felix; the plastic elephant that Stefan had owned since he was six; the hairbands that Kerstin liked to wear. She sat on the bed where Elisabeth Fritzl endured her violations year in, year out. She tried to imagine what it must have been like.

She wanted to feel her pain. But there could be no imagining it, not really.

Like soldiers returning from the trenches of the First World War, who said that no civilian could comprehend what they had been through in their bloody and mangled world, this confused, psychologically concussed old lady strove for a meaningful understanding, some sort of a connection to the terror which happened here. All it led to were tears and confusion. She felt she had failed, as she had failed in so many things in the 51 years she spent as the good and faithful wife of Josef Fritzl.

Rosemarie thought that seeing the place might act as some sort of catharsis, but it didn't; it just magnified her pain, her bewilderment. Doctors believe she is perhaps more damaged by the whole affair than anyone, including her daughter. Betrayed on every level by her spouse, she punishes herself for letting Elisabeth down. Letting herself down.

In that dripping, gloomy, dank, smelly grave that claimed the best years of the lives of her own flesh and blood, she sought answers, but only arrived back at the question that the whole world will ask in perpetuity: 'Why?'

In the last week of July, Rosemarie returned once more to the scene of her husband's great crime. She went with a car and a small trailer. A neighbour saw her.

'How are you doing?' she enquired.

'I'm OK,' Rosemarie replied. She was asked about all that had happened and where she was going, but would only say: 'A person who runs from their past will be on the run for ever.'

She went inside, collected some things, and drove them to a rented flat in Linz where she now lives. Her new life will be one spent removed from the man who stole so much: she has started divorce proceedings against him.

1 July, 2008

In the first week of July, in the grounds of a clinic, Felix is seen dancing around a tree, studying the ridges in the bark. He wears shoes with different-sized soles to help him cope with a strange condition caused by his existence in the cramped cellar. He walks strangely. He talks strangely. And when strangers speak to him he sometimes doesn't realize where the voices come from; until April this year the only strange voices he knew emanated from the TV set underground.

His skin is pale, although his sister Monika, seen playing with him, is tanned and healthy looking. Felix wears special lenses that darken in the sun – he is pale and doesn't have the round, healthy, sun-exposed face of his brother Alex.

The cellar children, and the upstairs clan, play with other children at the hospital in a private garden area made available to them by their therapists. It has a plastic swimming pool which, although just three metres wide, must seem like an ocean to those who have spent all their lives below ground. Felix has been given a bicycle, with stabilizer wheels at the back, which he is learning to ride. He has also learned to use a telephone – he misses his mother when she is away from their secure clinic home, when she is either making a statement to the police or having therapy – and she calls him often.

In the sunshine, everything looks bucolic and peaceful. Suddenly Felix picks up a blackbird feather and wants to know what it is. He gives it to his sister. She explains that it's from a bird, and they sit on a seat as she explains what she knows about birds – that they come from eggs and fly, and they live in trees. Felix has seen them on the TV, but never seen one before, not a live one. A free one.

Now he has a feather. Evidence of a real bird! He's then seen eating a fresh bread roll – healthy, wholegrain bread – not the insipid frozen bread he had in the cellar. He loves freshly baked bread. Then he's allowed to run ahead of his aunt, a visitor today, to the car park to look at the cars where he caresses their bonnets as if they were precious jewels.

It is summer. Truly, for Felix, it is a wonderful, wonderful world and one in which he, like his family, deserves to be happy, healthy and loved.

In forgetting where he came from he may be instrumental in healing not only his own wounds but also those of an awesome mother and an incredibly courageous brother and sister who endured to adulthood in the netherworld of a monster.

Acknowledgements

My thanks go to the following people for their invaluable help in the research and writing of this book: Mario Gavenda, David R. Hill, Thomas Hochwarter and Lisa Zoder. My thanks also go to Joerg Michner for organizing the photographs.

He just wanted a decent book to read ...

Not too much to ask, is it? It was in 1935 when Allen Lane, Managing Director of Bodley Head Publishers, stood on a platform at Exeter railway station looking for something good to read on his journey back to London. His choice was limited to popular magazines and poor-quality paperbacks – the same choice faced every day by the vast majority of readers, few of whom could afford hardbacks. Lane's disappointment and subsequent anger at the range of books generally available led him to found a company – and change the world.

'We believed in the existence in this country of a vast reading public for intelligent books at a low price, and staked everything on it'
Sir Allen Lane, 1902–1970, founder of Penguin Books

The quality paperback had arrived – and not just in bookshops. Lane was adamant that his Penguins should appear in chain stores and tobacconists, and should cost no more than a packet of cigarettes.

Reading habits (and cigarette prices) have changed since 1935, but Penguin still believes in publishing the best books for everybody to enjoy. We still believe that good design costs no more than bad design, and we still believe that quality books published passionately and responsibly make the world a better place.

So wherever you see the little bird – whether it's on a piece of prize-winning literary fiction or a celebrity autobiography, political tour de force or historical masterpiece, a serial-killer thriller, reference book, world classic or a piece of pure escapism – you can bet that it represents the very best that the genre has to offer.

Whatever you like to read – trust Penguin.